New World Architecture

Christian Norberg-Schulz

A series of three lectures presented at The Architectural League of New York on November 3, 5, and 10, 1987. These talks are the first J. Clawson Mills Lectures on American Architecture and Landscape.

D0911486

The Architectural League of New York
Princeton Architectural Press

An Architectural League
Publication

Kevin C. Lippert, Publisher
Anne Rieselbach, Managing Editor
Michael Bierut, Vignelli Associates, Designer
Ann C. Urban, Copy Editor

ISBN 0-910413-43-6

Published and distributed by
Princeton Architectural Press
37 East 7th Street
New York, New York 10003
212-995-9620

This book was printed and bound by Princeton University Press,
Princeton, NJ.

The Architectural League of New York
457 Madison Avenue
New York, New York 10022

Cover: New England Village, early 19th century, detail.
Courtesy National Gallery of Art, Washington; Gift of Edgar
William and Bernice Chrysler Garbisch.

Library of Congress, Cataloging-in-Publication Data

Norberg-Schulz, Christian.
  New world architecture.

  "A series of three lectures presented at the Architectural League
of New York on November 3, 5, and 10, 1987. These talks are
the first J. Clawson Mills lectures on American architecture and
landscape."
  1. Architecture—United States—Themes, motives.
I. Title.
NA705.N67   1988   720'.973   88-17834
ISBN 0-910413-43-6

Contents

Foreword

I

The three lectures contained in this book were first presented in 1987 at the Architectural League of New York as the J. Clawson Mills Lectures in American Architecture and Landscape.

The Architectural League was founded over one hundred years ago as a meeting place and a forum for the expression and discussion of ideas about architecture and the related arts. We have been amply assisted in this purpose by the J. Clawson Mills bequest, which created a fund whose proceeds are shared equally by the Architectural League and the Metropolitan Museum of Art and are used for scholarly purposes. Through the years the League has relied on this bequest to fund special projects, exhibitions, research, and public symposia, including "200 Years of American Architectural Drawing," "Collaboration: Artists and Architects," and a history of the Architectural League.

Last year we set aside a portion of the Mills Fund to provide an annual scholarship dedicated to the exploration and development of original ideas and the communication of these ideas within the architectural community. The scholarship makes possible research, study, and travel over a year's time on a specific theme of interest to the League. We defined our need, apart from other scholarly institutions that provide similar grants, as the presentation of studies of value to architects practicing today. In this definition we have perhaps eliminated the deep scholarly analysis of theoretical positions that are appropriately within the purview of other scholarly institutions and have sought, instead, new perceptions of our collective work and history that could illuminate the sources and sites of the creative process that is our daily fare. We have begun by seeking themes that help us to understand the world around us, the common ground we share, and what it is we create. In doing this we have sought a gentle redefinition of who we are and what we might become.

We have given particular care to the selection of the first Mills Scholar, knowing well that our choice of person as well as topic would set the tone for what we do hope will be an annual event. We were therefore delighted that Christian Norberg-Schulz agreed to accept our invitation to study American architecture and landscape.

II.

Christian Norberg-Schulz was born in Norway in 1926 and received a diploma in architecture from the Swiss Federal Polytechnic in Zurich, where he studied with Sigfried Giedion. He also studied at Harvard on a Fulbright scholarship. He has practiced architecture in Oslo and in Rome and has taught for over twenty years at the Oslo School of Architecture, where he was until last year the dean of the school. He has lectured widely around the world and received many honors in recognition of his achievements. This summer he received the Criticism and Teaching Prize of the International Union of Architects, which he shared with Ada Louise Huxtable.

He has written twenty books, including major historical works on Baroque architecture, Late Baroque, and Rococo architecture, and the architecture of Norway. His theoretical works, including *Intentions in Architecture, Existence, Space and Architecture, Meaning in Western Architecture, Genius Loci,* and *The Concept of Dwelling,* have developed the consistent point of view that architecture evokes, embodies, and transmits meaning, that architecture gives man an existential foothold, and that it is through the understanding of the simple everyday elements around us that we can gain an understanding of the whole.

His works have provided, for many of us practicing today, the beginning of an understanding of how to create buildings that are of the place, how to create a seamless environment in which architecture exists in relation to cities, to landscapes, and to man, and his words begin to tell us how to create a seamless tapestry of past, present, and future. Professor Norberg-Schulz has maintained a continuing interest in America since his days at Harvard through his conversations with Mies van der Rohe and Louis Kahn, his teaching at Yale University and the Massachusetts Institute of Technology, and his lectures, which have frequently brought him here.

He is that rarest of rare phenomena, the educated European who maintains an enthusiasm for our own primitive American culture.

It is our hope that the themes set forth in these lectures will guide and inspire our continuing creative search.

Frances Halsband
President, The Architectural League of New York

To generations of Europeans the very word "America" was synonymous with the dream of freedom and opportunity, and the history of the United States is the tale of how that dream became reality. Today the peoples of western Europe no longer suffer oppression and starvation, and the possibility of emigration has in any case almost disappeared. Still Europeans continue to go "over there," no longer going in search of freedom but rather, to find inspiration. In the past, Americans looked to the Old World for knowledge; today the situation is reversed, and Europeans come to the New World to learn.

Why is this so? The reason is simply that for 350 years the United States has experienced the possibilities and problems of freedom[1] thus laying the foundation for the modern, "open" world. This world is today a global reality, and therefore there is a great deal we can and should learn from the American experience.

What are the characteristics of the new state of affairs? An obvious one is the adoption of American products and way of life. More important, however, is the pluralism that is becoming increasingly universal. When we visit cities such as London and Paris today, we are immediately struck by the mixed color of the population, and even in more remote places such as Oslo or Helsinki, we encounter the same phenomenon. The American melting pot is evidently being extended to the whole world, and we remember Thomas Paine's prophetic words, "The cause of America is in a great measure the cause of all mankind."[2]

The word "freedom," used here as a key to the new situation, needs further explanation. First,it implies the possibility of choice. In past societies, the role and position of the individual was in general determined *a priori* as part of an integrated, static system. This state of affairs was particularly evident in the Middle Ages. With the Reformation, however, the closed European world opened up, and a certain element of choice became possible. The idea of system was not abandoned; but the systems multiplied, and the individual could, to some extent, choose where he wanted to go. In our context, then, "freedom" implies an "open" world, distinguished by movement, opportunity, and choice.[3] The colonization of America was the most important result of this new situation.

The modern world is, above all, an open world. Today we do not only live in a cosmopolitan situation, but as a rule we participate in the life of the entire globe. Daily the media bring us "news" from everywhere, and the conditions of distant places are no longer foreign to us. We experience a simultaneity of places rather than the traditional feeling of belonging to one particular place. A new dynamism has therefore been introduced into our perception of the environment.[4] As is well known, the open world came into being with the new means of production and communication that developed in the nineteenth century and has grown ever since. In general it implies that the memories and ideas of all cultures are now available to everybody.

But freedom also means that we want to liberate ourselves from these past memories and ideas and thus be allowed a new start. A new start implies somehow a return to "beginnings," that is, to what is basic and general. This aim is perhaps the primary characteristic of America and is contained in the very concept of a New World. One of its most recent manifestations is Louis Kahn's "love of beginnings" and his wish to read what he called "Volume Zero" of history.[5]

The modern world is thus distinguished by the demand for a new start at the same time as all the experiences of the past are available. America satisfied this demand, offering, in the words of Daniel Boorstin, "the first great opportunity . . . for men who had the accumulated culture, techniques, and mistakes of Europe behind them, to show the prosperity and effectiveness of the species, in a rich, a vast, and an unspoiled environment."[6]

The culture and techniques brought along by the immigrants, however, originally belonged to another context, and we cannot simply assume that they were still meaningful in America. An important question that ought to be answered by America, therefore, is what happens to forms that are transferred from one place to another? An obvious effect of such a transfer is fragmentation and relativization. The New World, in fact, no longer consists of integrated systems based on defined values but has become a seemingly chaotic multitude of scattered bits. Thus it makes the possibility of choice manifest.

The question then arises: How can man find a foothold in an open world of bits and fragments? In the past, economic and psychological security were offered by the system, although security often became synonymous with oppression. Today we are free but have lost the bases of past cultures. In other words, the bits do not constitute meaningful wholes. Again we describe a typical American situation: in America each thing is a separate, individual entity that must manage alone. Man is, for instance, no longer supported by a society in the traditional sense but must stand on his own feet.[7] To understand what this implies, we can make an analogy with spoken language. In the past, words such as "man," "earth," "heaven," and "God" were parts of systems of meanings and were understood in their context. Today such generally accepted contexts are no longer established, and what remains of the old systems has to a large extent been subject to disintegration and devaluation. Thus the words also tend to stand alone. Does this imply that they lose their meaning? Evidently not. They are still part of the (English) language, and their expressive possibilities are thereby determined. When we, for instance, say "house," something comes to our mind rather than nothing, and this something implies a particular identity. We may even say that the factual isolation of a thing means that it must be more itself; it has to possess a higher quality, since "quality" means that which something in reality "is."[8] Again we return to the beginnings, in the sense of the original meaning of the word as the naming of a recognized identity. Thus history can be understood as a series of interpretations of something that has "always been,"[9] rather than a collection of circumstantial traditions.

When we today turn to America, it is to learn how to live in an open world of individual bits. We want to find out how Americans have been able to understand and interpret the quality of things, and possibly how a choice between qualities may create an "island of meaning" in a seemingly chaotic environment of possibilities. Again we recall Thomas Paine, who said that America is "destined to be the primitive and precious model of what is to change the condition of man over the globe."[10]

How, then, do we relate these general points to architecture? In architectural terms, to gain a foothold in an open world still means to create places where private and public life take place. The forms of these places, however, will be different from those of past cultures and epochs. Whereas the character of a place in the past was distinct and memorable, today it tends to be complex and controversial. But it also expresses the demand for a return to beginnings, for something generally valid. What we encounter are "islands of meaning" rather than a comprehensive order. These islands, however, may have something in common if they all interpret the beginnings or, in other words, are constituted by elements from the same basic language of architecture.

The history of American architecture offers valuable information as to the nature of this language. It tells us that a new start, in terms of architecture, means first the creation of a new dwelling. In any world, closed or open, the house is what primarily satisfies man's need for a foothold, and my first task is to define the house of the modern world using the American experience as a source of inspiration. In a world where each individual stands alone, the house is particularly significant. In such a free world, however, man's actions also gain new weight. Each individual man must create his own world, and the result depends on his "power and success as Workman."[11] In the open world, therefore, the place of work is the building task that comes next to the house in importance. Accordingly, the *city* is understood as a collection of "nodes of activity," rather than an organism consisting of landmarks and squares. My second task is to discuss the city of the modern world in terms of its buildings and spatial organization. Again the American experience offers vital information. I have, moreover, suggested that the islands of meaning represented by houses, buildings, and urban ensembles must have something in common to be able to function as messages within the open world, and that this implies a *basic* language of architecture. My third task therefore is to discuss the American use of architectural forms in order to find out whether the notion of beginnings makes sense, and how it relates to the given forms that were transferred from somewhere else. In general the aim of this study is to arrive at a better comprehension of the architecture of our time, assuming that America represents the "primitive and precious model" of the modern open world. The basic question is to understand how bits of architecture may be composed to express meaning.

The title, *New World Architecture,* has a double meaning, therefore. First, it refers to America as the New World, but second, it implies that the new world of today needs an architecture that may possibly be inspired by the American experience. It has to be emphasized, however, that the American and the global situation are not analogous. The traditional civilizations of the Old World still possess a different historical dimension, although they are becoming increasingly open and cosmopolitan. They are not new in the American sense, but seen in a global perspective, each of them may be considered an "island of meaning" within a comprehensive situation. This repeats the American condition on a larger scale. *New World Architecture,* thus, means an architecture that developed in the United States and that today returns to the Old World, transforming its traditions in accordance with the open condition of modern man.

The House

1

1.
Ashley House, Old Deerfield,
MA, early 18th century.

In the conclusion to his book on the Shingle Style, Vincent Scully writes that, "America consequently produced her most original monuments where one after all might have expected to find them: in the homes of individual men." He adds, "Behind the whole development of free design ran the insistent belief that man must live as a free human being, in close contact with nature, in order to realize his own potentialities."[12] We see, thus, that freedom in terms of architecture means, first of all, the right to possess a dwelling, and that the detached house is the first manifestation of the open world. How then were these houses intended and built? Did they express man's individuality as such, or did they demonstrate his need for a return to beginnings?

The early houses of New England and Virginia were certainly based on models imported from England, a fact often described and explained.[13] Yet some important questions remain to be answered. First, the use of a particular model always implies a choice, and second, the transfer of anything to a new place necessitates some kind of adaptation. If we take a look at these early houses, it is strikingly evident that they represent a certain type. This type was chosen among several possible alternatives from the Old World, and when it "settled" in the New World it both became more precise and, through variations, was adapted to the different circumstances in New England and Virginia. The primary typical properties of this type are the symmetrical disposition of the plan and the main (entrance) facade and the simple and easily comprehensible general form distinguished by a gable roof with eaves close to the wall. The examples are legion. In current literature, the Parson Capen House in Topsfield, Massachusetts, is often cited as a kind of prototype (1683), while the Adam Thoroughgood House represents the first Virginia dwellings (1636–1640).[14] Both houses are approximately symmetrical and have a pronounced figural quality. We could add to these almost any colonial house from the seventeenth and eighteenth centuries. A group of beautiful, well-preserved specimens are standing in Old Deerfield, Massachusetts, and the reconstructed townscape of Williamsburg is marked by a basically similar type.

English models certainly exist,[15] but the typological identity of the early American house cannot simply be explained as a colonial echo. In general the English vernacular is distinguished by a freer and more picturesque formal treatment than the strict organization we find in America. In England symmetrical facades are an exception rather than a rule, and the main form is often obscured by various kinds of projections

and additions.[16] In New England additions to the
houses were generally solved as lean-tos at the back
of the houses, resulting in the characteristic saltbox
section. As a consequence, the symmetrical facade is
preserved while the rear becomes an informal place
in contact with nature. The obvious wish for a distinct
figural form cannot be explained in functional terms.
If the colonial house had been intended as a strong-
hold offering protection against attack, for instance, it
would have had quite a different shape.[17] The simple
box-like volume and the symmetrical facade are qualities offering psychological security instead, first by de-
fining a distinct "here" and second by representing
the "individual man." In Puritan New England, the
wish for order also expressed the concept of a
controlled and decent way of life.

The basic qualities of these early houses are common
to Virginia and New England, although the interpretations of the basic themes differ somewhat with the
background of the settlers and the given environment.
In New England the house developed as part of a village and mostly stayed small in scale, which suited
the differentiated topography of the land. In Virginia,
on the contrary, the house became the center of an in-
dependent plantation, located in the extended and
uniform landscape of the Tidewater region. As a result it grew in size, without losing its basic figural
quality, however—as is well illustrated by Westover
(1730–1734).[18] The basic intentions are already
manifest in Bacon's Castle, c. l655, but with picturesque English memories still present, which were
subsequently abandoned in favor of more archetypal
forms. Some of the English elements, however,
lingered on in Virginia, such as exterior chimneys on
the gable walls and pointed dormers. But again, there
is a basic difference in the use of these elements in
Virginia. In England they are generally freely placed
and form part of a picturesque composition. In America, on the contrary, they serve to emphasize the
figural quality of the house. Exterior chimneys do not
appear in New England, but we do find a regular dis-
tribution of the secondary elements.

The interiors of the early houses show an analogous
wish for archetypal dualities. The rooms are usually
symmetrical, centered on a large fireplace; they are
covered by a powerful timber structure, where chimney girt and summer beam establish the regular spatial order. When George Washington explained his
plans for the new dining room at Mount Vernon in
1776, he wrote, "The chimney of the new room
should be exactly in the middle of it—the doors and
everything else to be exactly answereable [sic] and

2.
The Solomon Richardson
House ca. 1748, on its original
site in East Brookfield, MA.
The building was relocated in
the 1940's to Old Sturbridge Village, Sturbridge, MA.
3.
Westover, Charles City Co., VA,
c. 1730–34.

uniform . . . ."[19] Within this regular space, however, the position of the furniture was not fixed, in contrast to so many European farmers' houses. Thus the furnishings expressed a new freedom of movement and meaning, and as time passed, the interiors tended to become "museums" of personal memories, rather than the manifestation of a particular tradition.

The early houses of Virginia and New England show that from the beginning American architecture established a language of basic forms and types.[20] The unconscious aim evidently was to contribute to the cultural identity of the New World. The basic forms, be they the symmetrical facade, ornate entrance, or large fireplace, were something more than status symbols; they were distinct *images,* giving the settlers a simultaneous sense of freedom and success. Thus the American house shows that freedom does not mean arbitrary self-expression but rather, the right to possess something of general value. In Europe such values were reserved for the few; in America they became, at least in principle, within the reach of everyone.

Although vernacular in character, the strict organization of the early houses may be understood as the expression of a hidden Classicism, and the general values implied naturally favored the direct introduction of classical elements and motifs. In the third part of this study, I will return to the meaning of the classical language, but I must point out now that, from the start, American architecture was classically oriented. The use of classical forms in the public buildings of Williamsburg around 1700 is hardly representative of this tendency, but during the following century, classical motifs appear on the facades and in the interiors of common dwellings.

In Old Deerfield, Massachusetts, a series of beautiful, well-preserved houses show how classical elements were used to emphasize the figural quality of the general composition.[21] This was done through simple door surrounds, small pediments over the windows, and a slightly projecting cornice. Evidently the aim was not to create a fully articulate classical organism like the pattern-book works of Peter Harrison from the same period[22] but rather, to introduce memories that somehow humanize the elementary, box-like house at the same time as they prepare one for the interior. In Deerfield we encounter a further definition of the typical, quasi-symmetrical space by means of fielded paneling or regularly placed pilasters. An analogous difference between the outside and the inside is found in Virginia, for example in Stratford Hall (1725–1730), where the splendid Great Hall is

4

5

4.
Parson Capen House, Topsfield, MA, 1683, parlor.
5.
Stratford Hall, Westmoreland County, VA, c. 1725–30.

experienced as a kind of revelation after the austere solidity of the exterior. An interaction between the two domains is, however, suggested by Stratford's H-shaped plan, and a new kind of feeling for nature is thereby brought forth.

This new sense of nature determines the further development of the American house during the second half of the eighteenth century. It is not surprising that this development took place in Virginia where the great houses of the plantations served as gathering centers to the surrounding land. Westover and Shirley already express their relative positions on the James River,[23] and in George Washington's Mount Vernon, the enclosed house for the first time opens up to communicate with the surroundings. The striking new feature introduced at Mount Vernon is the high-pillared "piazza" that extends the length of the house. This piazza both adapts the house to the setting and emphasizes its figural quality. It was a creative use of the classical colonnade, indeed, which became one of the distinctive motifs of American architecture. The simple entablature deprives the porch of any exaggerated monumentality; the result is rather a kind of democratic greatness that well expresses the character of the new nation. The "piazza" was erected in 1777, the year after the Declaration of Independence. A weather vane added in 1787 emphasizes the small cupola, making the meaning of the house as a "center" manifest. At Mount Vernon, thus, the private realm of the house interacts with the public space of the land, as pointed out by Robert A.M. Stern.[24]

What was suggested by George Washington was developed and accomplished by Thomas Jefferson. In Jefferson's work an American Classicism is realized, which remains one of the greatest achievements of the history of American architecture. Starting from a deep understanding of the qualities of nature, Jefferson revived the original contents of classical architecture and brought a new dimension of meaning into the American environment. It is well known that he aimed at a break with English architecture. As early as 1760, while he was a student in Williamsburg, he had already begun to criticize the buildings he saw there; and after a two-month trip to England in 1786, he wrote: "English architecture is in the most wretched stile I ever saw, not meaning to except America where it is bad, nor even Virginia where it is worse than in any other part of America, which I have seen."[25] What he did then was to return to the classical sources in order to discover "the first principles of the art."[26]

6.
Stratford Hall, Great Hall.
7.
Mount Vernon, Fairfax Co.,
VA, 1757–87.

8.
*Monticello, Charlottesville, VA,
Thomas Jefferson, 1793–1809.*
9.
*Monticello, surrounding land-
scape.*
10.
Monticello.

9

10

With his search for the universal, Jefferson combined a love of nature, that is, of the concrete "here." In addition he was certainly a practical American and liked to work with his hands. The choice of the site for his own house, Monticello, proves that his poetical interests were stronger than his utilitarian sense. As the name indicates, Monticello is located on the top of a "small mountain," with difficult access and limited possibilities for agriculture. From his mountain, however, Jefferson could overlook the surrounding land and feel at the center of a microcosmos that represented the whole of America; at the same time he could experience the concrete phenomena of nature. Thus he wrote: "Where has Nature spread so rich a mantle under the eye? Mountains, rocks, rivers. With what majesty do we there ride above the storms! How sublime to look down into the workhouse of nature, to see her clouds, hail, snow, rain, thunder, all fabricated at our feet! And the glorious Sun, when rising as if out of a distant water, just gilding the top of the mountains and giving life to all nature!"[27] Here American freedom transcends the original rights for work and religious participation and is extended to include the right for experience and understanding. It is certainly no coincidence that this richer approach was introduced by the man who wrote the Declaration of Independence.

In his house, as it was built between 1793 and 1809, Jefferson set his vision and aims to work. At first sight Monticello appears to be in the Palladian tradition, and it certainly owes much to the Italian master and to the Venetian villas in general. At closer acquaintance, however, differences become evident that distinguish the house as a truly American creation. The active contact with the surroundings due to the use of porches, bay windows, and terraces is certainly a manifestation of American freedom, as are the differentiated and articulate rooms inside. Monticello is not intended for representation, like so much of the European upper-class domestic architecture, but is first of all livable, in the sense of combining identity of place with richness of experience. The experiences do not primarily consist of a spontaneous perception of natural phenomena, but rather a deeper understanding made possible by the architecture. Thus the house becomes a "museum of the soul" and a true work of art.[28]

Compared with the simple box-like dwellings of the early settlers, Monticello appears as a differentiated and complex organism. Still, it preserves the basic figural identity of the early houses. This is due not only to the symmetrical layout but also to the continuous entablature and superposed balustrade that run around the whole building. Within this general coherence, classical columns and pediments are used to define directions and places. The point of departure is not the wish for creating an articulate, plastic *body* of the traditional classical kind but to define a composition of *spaces*.[29] The open world of America was thereby expressed; it was understood and visualized for the first time, suggesting that the closed colonial epoch had come to an end, and a new period of expansion had begun. Monticello incorporates what Scully calls the "two deep-seated compulsions, both always very apparent in America, one seeking rootedness and protection, the other demanding freedom and mobility";[30] and, to quote Scully again, it also expresses "a struggle between the fixed European past and the mobile American future, between Palladio and Frank Lloyd Wright, between a desire for contained, classical geometry and an instinct to spread out horizontally along the surface of the land."[31] We understand that the struggle between the two compulsions contains the very problem of freedom, and that the equilibrium obtained at Monticello represents an eminently satisfactory solution. We could also say that Monticello is the first case of the "destruction of the box" wanted by Frank Lloyd Wright one hundred years later. Jefferson's primary purpose, however, was still to create a defined "here."

The further development of the classical house culminates with the Greek Revival. In the 1830's and 40's, innumerable houses with pronounced temple facades were built in the United States. They were the result of a genuine interest in ancient Greek democracy in connection with the Greek War for Independence and undoubtedly contributed to diffuse a sense of quality and style among the population. Preserving the demand for figural identity, they did not interrupt the American tradition; but neither did they contribute much to its further development, with the exception perhaps of the plantation house of the deep South, where the giant colonnade introduced by Washington came to surround the entire building, creating a relationship between outside and inside suitable to the climate of the region. In general the Greek Revival established the idea of the [gabled] house as the temple of the family, expressing thus another aspect of American democracy.

The sense of nature, so important to Jefferson, changed during the nineteenth century into a different, romantic approach. The former view sought basic enviromental characters (in the Greek sense), but the latter aimed at grasping nuances and moods. Thus

11

11.
Levi Lincoln House, Sturbridge,
MA, 1820.

12

12.
House in Massachusetts, latter
19th century.

Emerson wrote: "Not the sun or the summer alone, but every hour and season yields its tribute of delight; for every hour and change corresponds to and authorizes a different state of the mind . . .,"[32] and: "Not less excellent . . . was the charm, last evening, of a January sunset. The western clouds divided and subdivided themselves into pink flakes modulated with tints of unspeakable softness; and the air had so much life and sweetness, that it was a pain to come within doors."[33] What kind of architecture would arise from such an approach to the environment? Hardly the classical, composed, unitary volume that symmetrically affronts the world. But the large fireplace might remain, as well as the bay window—the two places of inward and outward contemplation.

The romantic approach in fact produced a new architecture known as the Picturesque.[34] The source of inspiration was no longer the classical orders and principles but was instead the Gothic world of complex and irregular shapes. A Gothic Revival resulted, and the house became asymmetrical and differentiated into wings, pavilions, verandas, and towers. Other modes of expression also came into use, and towards the end of the century, an almost limitless pluralism of styles was prevalent. Although the Picturesque took a genuine interest in nature as its point of departure, it was ever more put at the service of individual self-expression. Thus the theorist of the Picturesque, Andrew Jackson Downing, wrote: "The villa . . . should above all things, manifest individuality. It should say something of the character of the family within . . ." and acordingly may be built "in any one of a dozen styles . . . ."[35] We understand that American freedom had at this time entered a new phase. What had been the freedom of choice had become the myth of success, and the pursuit of happiness had become the pursuit of wealth.[36] The Picturesque movement, in fact, culminated with the "Dream Houses" of Vanderbilt and Hearst.[37]

In spite of the evident dangers of degeneration implicit in picturesque architecture, it offered a significant contribution to the development of the American house. The asymmetrical organization of space presaged the "free plan" of Modernism and the picturesque composition of open and closed volumes its collage-like forms. Particular elements such as continuous porches, extended areas of glass, and skeletal structure also became constituent facts for later developments. These qualities are first found in the varieties of the Picturesque known as the Stick Style and the Shingle Style.[38] While the Stick Style was part of an international current, taking the Swiss vernacular as its point of departure, the Shingle Style is genuinely American. It is interesting to note that the Stick Style was due to a conscious attempt to create an architecture of freedom. In the nineteenth century, Switzerland was looked upon as the first democratic country in Europe, and its folk architecture accordingly became a model for numerous national romantic movements.[39]

The Shingle Style is related to the Stick Style in its treatment of space; but as a rule the volumes are simpler, and the continuous shingle covering creates a strong sense of unity. A reference to the houses of the early settlers is thereby obtained as well as a combination of the original wish for figural identity with the new spatial freedom. The outstanding example usually cited is the William G. Low House in Bristol, Rhode Island, by McKim, Mead and White (1887, demolished in the early 1960's). Here a rich ensemble of porches and bay windows were controlled by a single dominant gable. As pointed out by Scully, the Shingle Style also arrived at a new definition of archetypal elements: "the massive platform, the precise posts, the solemn gable."[40] These characteristics are especially evident in the houses of Bruce Price from about 1885. In Price's houses, we also find a successful combination of traditional American symmetry with the new wish for volumetric differentiation.

As a more personal interpretation of the Picturesque, I ought to mention the John J. Glessner House in Chicago, by Henry Hobson Richardson (1885). The house is entirely of stone, in Richardson's highly personalized interpretation of the Romanesque, known today as "Richardsonian Romanesque."[41] It may seem all new but is in reality a new interpretation of the early American dwelling, with a symmetrical two-story facade on the main street and a secondary outshot added along the side. The enclosing formality of the front and the more open character towards the court are also in accordance with the American tradition. The deep understanding of basic values that distinguishes the house is well expressed by the story of how the "domestic fire" was brought along from the Glessner's old house when moving into the new one.[42]

Located in Chicago, the Glessner House demonstrates that the domestic architecture of the Midwest that developed after the Civil War did not ignore the American tradition. But the time and the place were different. A new dynamism had come about, and a more aggressive attitude to human life demanded another interpretation of the values of freedom and openness.

13

14

15

13.
William G. Low House, Bristol, RI, McKim, Mead and White, 1887.
14.
John J. Glessner House, Chicago, IL, Henry Hobson Richardson, 1885. Photograph c. 1888.
15.
Glessner House, courtyard.

This interpretation was accomplished by Frank Lloyd Wright, and it is not accidental that he called his architecture the Prairie Style. With the Great Plains, a new kind of environment had been discovered, a truly open, limitless world that more than anything known before corresponded to the aims of the New World. Let William Cullen Bryant describe the prairie to us:

These are the gardens of the Desert, these
The unshorn fields, boundless and beautiful,
For which the speech of England has no name—
The Prairies. I behold them for the first,
And my heart swells while the dilated sight
Takes in the encircling vastness. Lo, they stretch
In airy undulations, far away . . . (1832).[43]

Frank Lloyd Wright translated this perception into architectural terms, saying: "We of the Middle West are living on the prairie. The prairie has a beauty of its own and we should recognize and accentuate this natural beauty, its quiet level. Hence, gently sloping roofs, low proportions, quiet skylines, suppressed heavy-set chimneys, and sheltering overhangs, low terraces and out-reaching walls sequestering private gardens."[44] The prairie, thus, is essentially open expanse and therefore needs an architecture of horizontal movement, which simultaneously expresses liberating openness and the need for a foothold on infinity. Wright's answer was "low proportions" and "out-reaching walls" but also "heavy-set chimneys" and "sheltering overhangs."

The grammar of Wright's architecture is well known. In the literature on the subject it is usually presented as something radically new, and his destruction of the box by means of outreaching walls and continuous band windows was certainly a new aim. But we also know that he had his predecessors. Giedion has pointed out that Wright's cruciform plan, with a centrally placed chimney stack and exterior porches, was derived from a well-known type of nineteenth-century standard house,[45] and it also appears in Jefferson's first design for Monticello (1768–70).[46] The desire to integrate a house with its natural surroundings leads to certain archetypal patterns of spatial organization. The powerful, centrally placed chimney stack is another archetypal means, having the purpose of tying the house to the ground; the fireplace also represents one of the fundamental values of natural, democratic life. The domestic fire of the Glessner House again comes to our mind, recalling Wright's own words, "It comforted me to see the fire burning deep in the solid masonry of the house itself."[47] Rather than a retreat, Wright intended the house as a fixed point in space from which man could experience a new sense of freedom and participation, as well as a "deeper sense of reality." Thus he expressed his own identity as a "child of the ground and of space."[48]

The houses of Wright's "first golden age"[49] show that he indeed worked within the American tradition, although he aimed at a new departure. His own Oak Park home, as originally built (1889), was dominated by an embracing solemn gable and centered on an inglenook on the axis of the composition. Even more American than the Oak Park home, is the famous Winslow House in River Forest (1893), with its symmetrical representative facade and informal back side where the rooms communicate actively with the garden. The plan is evidently derived from the early New England houses. The same basic traits appear over and over again in the following years, although the increasing destruction of the box tends to obscure the simple, underlying order. Wright's compositions, however, never become arbitrarily irregular; they are always based on a hidden classical geometry and thus continue the pursuit initiated by Jefferson at Monticello. Thanks to this geometrical organization and the precise definition of the elements, Wright's early houses possess a strong figural quality. As an example, consider the much admired Isabel Roberts House in River Forest (1908). Here a quasi-symmetrical cruciform plan is controlled by a two-story volume centered on a large fireplace. Openness is the overriding principle due to the use of outreaching walls, deep overhangs, and continuous clerestories, but at the same time the house appears as a protecting shelter anchored to the ground. It is one of the great interpretations of American freedom and a point of departure for the New World architecture of the twentieth century.

In 1910 and 1911, Wright's works were published in Germany and caused a revolution in European architectural thinking and practice.[50] An important difference in approach is nonetheless evident. Whereas Wright's houses always were intended as concrete places, realized by means of natural materials and quasi-figurative elements, the European dwellings inspired by his grammar tended toward abstract juxtapositions of horizontal and vertical planes without any reference to archetypal values. This is particularly obvious in Gerrit Rietveld's Schroeder House in Utrecht (1924), as well as in Mies van der Rohe's early works.[51] The latter exhibit a comprehensive geometrical order visualized as a regular skeleton of steel columns, but the order is general and abstract and basically different from the concrete directions and

16

17

16.
Winslow House, River Forest, IL, Frank Lloyd Wright, 1893.
17.
Isabel Roberts House, River Forest, IL, Frank Lloyd Wright, 1908.

axes of Wright's plans. The *livable* quality of the American houses was lost in Europe.

In the 1930's, the new European architecture, inspired by Frank Lloyd Wright, was exported back to America. The exhibition entitled "Modern Architecture, International Exhibition," held at the Museum of Modern Art in 1932, marked the new situation, and a few years later Walter Gropius and Marcel Breuer arrived as refugees from Nazi Germany. Today it is rather embarrassing to read Hitchcock and Johnson's eulogy of the International Style and their criticism of Wright as a "rebel" and an "individualist."[52] Their judgment, however, corresponds to the situation in 1931—the tradition in architecture that we had followed from the days of the early settlers had been interrupted, and a new abstract approach to the problem of human dwelling had taken its place. We cannot discuss the reasons for this change here; it must suffice to suggest that it had to do with the devaluation of symbols of the "dream house" and also with a new belief in functionalism. During the thirties, however, most American architects continued to work in a somewhat diluted traditional vein, but the influence of Gropius and Breuer, and somewhat later of Mies van der Rohe, became increasingly important and after World War II came to dominate.

It would be unfair to reject the houses by Gropius, Breuer, and their followers as entirely foreign to America. As manifestations of modern, informal living, they were certainly related to some of the traditional American aims. In their works we also find several attempts at adapting to the local environment, for example through the use of white painted wooden siding or large fireplaces of rubble.[53] Today, however, these adaptations seem utterly naive, and we recognize that these European architects derailed American architecture. The general result was a multitude of so-called "houses" consisting of a characterless juxtaposition of non-figurative elements that neither belong to tradition nor respect the spirit of the place.[54] Mies van der Rohe's Farnsworth House (1946–51) is a rare exception, being a true, poetical interpretation of openness and freedom. Its source of inspiration, however, is more the urban architecture of the Chicago School than the American domestic tradition.

Although some of the modern dwellings of the postwar years satisfied the demand for informal living in contact with nature, they are not convincing as *houses*. A house is something more than a functional container. It ought to *look* like a house and thereby offer a sense of identity in space and time. In other

18

18.
Farnsworth House, Plano, IL,
Ludwig Mies van der Rohe,
1946-51.

words, the house has to possess what we have called figural quality. This quality is obtained when each element as well as the whole is a "nameable object."[55] In the third part of this study, I will return to this question but have here to say a few words about how a new generation of architects have succeeded in recovering the idea of "house" as a continuation of the American tradition.

The decisive step was taken by Robert Venturi with the Vanna Venturi House in Philadelphia (1962). The key to this house, and to Venturi's aims in general, is his concept of a "difficult whole." Venturi wants a "whole," in the sense of a "symbolic image of house," but today this whole has become "difficult" because it ought to accommodate the "complexities and contradictions" of modern life. Thus he combines the "symmetrical consistency of the outside" and an "originally symmetrical" plan with "circumstantial distortions."[56] The "difficulty" implicit in Venturi's house reflects the new complexity of the American situation. Although America always was an open society, the traditional idea of melting pot suggests that the aim of the past was to melt the differences into a common American mold. Today this aim has been superseded by pluralistic diversity, a situation initiated by the individualism of the post-Civil War period. We have already characterized this condition as a "world of separate bits." And still, the new, total openness needs the American tradition to gain a foothold. Venturi's house is in fact based on known models in its general disposition, and it also revives the idea of the dwelling as the "museum of the soul" (something quite different from arbitrary self-expression). The importance of Venturi's approach was recognized by Scully, who in the introduction to Venturi's *Complexity and Contradiction in Architecture* wrote: "This is surely Venturi's largest achievement in American terms, that he opens our eyes again to the nature of things as they are in the United States . . . and that out of our common, confused, mass produced fabric he makes a solid architecture; he makes an art. In so doing he revives the popular traditions, and the particularized methodology, of the pre-Beaux Arts, pre-International Style, period."[57]

Another pioneering effort in the same direction is represented by the works of Charles Moore, Donlyn Lyndon, William Turnbull, and Richard Whitaker, in particular at the Sea Ranch development on the northern California Coast (begun 1965). The aim of the group may be stated as the "creation of memorable places" and was explained in the significant book *The Place of Houses,* by Moore, Lyndon, and Gerald Allen.[58]

19.
Vanna Venturi house, Philadelphia, Robert Venturi, 1962.
20.
Sea Ranch, North of San Francisco, CA, MLTW, 1965ff.

The first chapters are dedicated to the American tradition, discussing two settlements from the past, Edgartown on Martha's Vineyard and Santa Barbara in Southern California, as well as Sea Ranch, which is understood as part of this historical development. After these case studies, *The Place of Houses* is laid out as a kind of pattern book. To explain the organization of the house plan, several traditional examples are analyzed: the Parson Capen House, the Gunston Hall from Virginia (1758), the Pringle House from Charleston (1774), the Homeplace Plantation from Louisiana (c. 1801), and the Ward Willitts house by Frank Lloyd Wright (1902). Stratford Hall is also cited in connection with the quality of its interior. What results is a kind of archetypal grammar, whose usefulness is proved in the included projects by the authors and their collaborators. Most of the projects, such as Sea Ranch itself, are distinguished by a convincing figural quality in relation to their site, and they certainly satisfy the wish for "memorable places."

The quest for the recovery of the house, however, does not end here. From 1965 on, Robert A.M. Stern has carried through a particularly systematic and significant exploration of the nature and varieties of the detached human dwelling and has managed to set his ideas into work in numerous projects that indeed deserve the name "house."[59] Stern's houses are for the most part large and expensive, but it would be superficial to use this as an argument against his general aims. Stern himself clearly explained his approach: "As I believe profoundly in the continuity of tradition, I search for the signs of its persistence in the present: I search the contemporary scene for icons of permanence and I do my best to use them in order to foster a sense of my work as an anchor in the effluvia of current production. I try to make the outward manifestations of change comprehensible by entering into a dialogue with the past, with tradition . . . . My attitude toward form, based on a love for and a knowledge of history, is not concerned with accurate replication. It is eclectic and uses collage and juxtaposition as techniques to give new meaning to familiar shapes."[60]

The Lang House in Connecticut (1973–74) illustrates Stern's ideas. Here a representative, symmetrical facade announces a subtly articulate plan based on a play of symmetries and asymmetries. Toward the landscape, the space opens up to create a rich sense of interaction between inside and outside. In general the house contains "everything." It is universal and local, traditional and modern; it reflects the experiences of the free plan, but gives the modern openness definition and coherence; even without furniture and

objects inside, it appears as a "museum of the soul," reflecting the architect's love for and knowledge of history.

In Stern's later houses numerous traditional elements appear: the lateral porch, the entrance porch, the classical column, the gable, the pediment, the dormer, the bay window, the exterior chimney, and the large fireplace—the nameable things of architectural history.[61]

Stern's approach is of general interest and represents an important contribution to the American experience. He recognizes that American culture is eclectic and moreover understands that this is becoming a general condition. He also recognizes the importance of the classical and the vernacular, that is, the relationship between what is general and what is local. Thus he helps our understanding of the nature and development of the open world. Like Venturi before him, he rejects Modernism as exclusive and considers it an insufficient answer to our present complexities.

The history of the American house is illuminating and significant. No other country can point to anything of equal importance. Only in Northern Europe do we find a similarly continuous tradition of domestic architecture, obviously because of the democratic and "natural" way of life in the Nordic countries. But in Northern Europe, the demands of the open world have so far been less apparent, and the houses have remained within conventional limits.

What then is the basic lesson offered by the American house? Summing up, we may say that it consists in the demonstration that a house is a concrete thing, possessing a distinct typological quality. Rooted in a particular place, it must be recognized and remembered for its figural properties. As a manifestation of an open world, however, it has to combine its basic identity with the capacity of incorporating circumstantial distortions and memories. Hence it both represents a return to beginnings, in Jefferson's sense of "the first principles of the art," and an awareness of the present. We can also say that the American house is simultaneously more archetypal and more modern than the houses of Old World traditions. In the American house, both the first principles and the particular memories are set into work as a nameable composition. Therefore, it shows us how to dwell in the New World.[62]

21.
Lang House, Washington, CT, Robert A.M. Stern, 1973-74.
22.
Residence, East Hampton, NY, Robert A.M. Stern, 1980-83.
23.
Monticello.

In *The Image of the City,* Kevin Lynch quotes an inhabitant of Los Angeles, who characterizes his city with these words, "It's as if you were going somewhere for a long time, and when you got there you discovered there was nothing there, after all."[63] Downtown Los Angeles has a typical American gridiron plan, and although this particular city spreads out more than perhaps any other, the judgment cited by Lynch could have been applied to almost any American town. "There was nothing there." The words confirm Lewis Mumford's evaluation of the grid: "in the gridiron plan, as applied in the commercial city, no section or precinct was suitably planned for its specific function: instead the only function considered was the progressive intensification of use . . . . Now the fact is that in urban planning, such bare surface order is no order at all."[64] Is, then, the American city a kind of non-place? When we do not arrive at any particular goal, but rather find ourselves within an indeterminate pattern, we evidently experience a condition that corresponds to what I have called the open world. Openness moreover implies change and therefore the impossibility of fixing specific functions. The question then arises: Is an open city still a place that can serve human life; that is, can it allow for orientation and identification?[65] Before we answer this question, however, we have to look at the historical development of the open city.

In the open city, the *street* becomes the primary fact, or more precisely, a street without definite ends and limits. The street has always been an expression of man's role as a *homo viator,* and as such it is an original architectural fact. "An axis is perhaps the first human manifestation; it is the means of every human act," Le Corbusier says. "The toddling child moves along an axis, the man striving in the tempest of life traces for himself an axis."[66] In the past, however, the axis or path led to a goal where the purpose of the movement was explained as part of a closed system of meanings. In the open city, movement gains a meaning in itself, and the street accordingly becomes a manifestation of opportunity and change or, in other words, of the American condition.

The open street has from the very beginning been a potential fact of American urbanism. With the term "potential fact," I suggest that the aim was always there, although it took time before it became fully realized. In Williamsburg (begun 1699) the straight main street, Duke of Gloucester Street, is a space 99 feet wide and about three-quarters of a mile long, lined by individual houses.[67] Although it has a public building at either end and a Market Square in the middle, there

24.
Williamsburg, Duke of Glouces-
ter Street, 1699ff.

25.
*New England Village, early
19th century.*

26

26.
Philadelphia, 1762.
27.
New Haven, 1748.

27

is hardly any feeling of an enclosed, urban space in the traditional European sense. Openness and contact with nature also characterize the wide, green avenue that leads to the Governor's Palace, crossing the main street at a right angle where the parish church is located. The plan of Williamsburg is laid out in relation to goals, but at the same time it expresses a new sense of infinite space. This characteristic is supported by the symmetrical facades of the houses, which do not form any continuous row but stand alone as individual identities. Models for the plan of Williamsburg may certainly be identified in the smaller towns and villages of England where we also find a green surrounded by houses, often with a church within or at one end of the green.[68] But in these English villages, the houses usually form continuous lines, and the place appears as an enclosed whole. Williamsburg, thus, undoubtedly indicates the beginning of a new kind of open urbanism.

The Puritan villages of New England also consist of separate houses around a green or a common containing the congregational meetinghouse. To secure the unity of the place, no one was allowed to live more than half a mile from the meetinghouse, and if the town grew beyond a certain size, a new settlement had to be founded[69] —a rule already known from the *polis* of Greek antiquity. Lewis Mumford points out that the New England village represents a medieval tradition, but it must be added that in spite of its unity, it possesses an openness hardly known in Europe. The contact with nature is outspoken, and the community consists of individuals rather than subjects. Thus the New England village also suggests a kind of anti-urban urbanism.

In 1638 New Haven was laid out on a gridiron plan, representing the first American town of its kind. The layout consists of nine equal squares; the middle one is a green with a meetinghouse at its center.[70] The affinity with the New England village is obvious, but in New Haven the potential openness of the village has been translated into an infinite, regular pattern. Again I may point to historical models, such as the Hippodamian cities of Greek Antiquity, but I must add that the American variety expresses another spirit. In 1682 William Penn planned Philadelphia on an analogous but much larger grid, and in 1733 Savannah followed a similar plan. The well-known engraving of Savannah from 1734 nicely illustrates the intended openness implicit in the grid plan, showing how the equal lots have been filled in in part with individual, symmetrical houses. During the nineteenth century, innumerable cities and villages in the Midwest,

Southwest, and West were laid out in the same manner, demonstrating a general accceptance of the grid principle.[71] The primary role of the street is evident, and it is interesting to notice that the central square is often occupied by a courthouse rather than a meeting-house, while various churches are located outside its periphery. A new pluralism thus becomes manifest.

In some cases, the presence of institutions of primary importance determined modifications of the grid pattern. This is particularly the case in Washington, D.C. L'Enfant's plan of 1791 incorporates two major axes that run east-west and north-south, crossing each other at a right angle as they meet the Potomac. The first axis has the Capitol as its "goal," the other the White House. The disposition is quite similar to the one in Williamsburg, as is the wide openness of the green spaces. New, however, is the "infinite" extension of the axes toward the south and the west, relating the city to a larger natural context. Also new is the introduction of diagonals that partly center the attention on the focal points and partly offer infinite vistas in the manner of Le Nôtre. In spite of its more articulate urban structure, Washington remains a manifestation of American openness. The Mall in particular does not possess the quality of an urban space but appears as an immense green.

In 1785 Congress decided that all the territory west of the Appalachians should be organized by an immense grid consisting of lines that run north-south and east-west and define six-mile squares. Each of these large squares was subdivided into thirty-six smaller squares. Thus the urban grid was used on natural and agricultural land,[72] and as a result, a large part of the United States appears as an immense checkerboard pattern when seen from the air. A plan of this kind is completely artificial and does not take topographical conditions into consideration. It does not respect nature as such and reverses the traditional relationship between what is natural and what is man-made. "Curved lines, you know," remarked a Cincinnati resident in 1794, "symbolize the country, straight lines the city."[73] In the past, in fact, the straight contours of man-made towns were found within the encompassing topological ground of nature, whereas in the planned part of the United States the natural elements are enclosed by the straight lines of the artificial grid.

This reversal of the traditional relationship clearly expresses man's desire to dominate nature, and it makes for frightening prospectives. It is therefore rather surprising to realize that Thomas Jefferson was one of the fathers of the plan. Evidently he did not see any

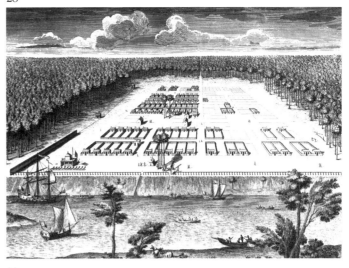

28.
Savannah, 1734.
29.
Washington, D.C., 1792.
30.
The Mall, Washington, D.C.

conflict between this kind of rationalism and the natural values he loved so deeply. Perhaps he even felt that the grid would bring nature closer to man, and he certainly regarded the plan as a symbolic manifestation of the open American world. The main motive behind the solution, however, was to offer everybody equal opportunities, and hence the rural grid has a democratic basis.

Hardly any other manifestation of the American approach to man's environment has caused more controversy than the grid. I have already quoted Lewis Mumford's criticism and may add that he explained it as an expression of a "capitalist regime."[74] An analogous interpretation is given by the Italian Mario Manieri-Elia, who considers the grid the result of, and condition for, a *laissez-faire* attitude.[75] Both commentaries may be correct, but I do not think that they cover the meaning of the grid as a physical manifestation of the open world. As such, the grid is not evil; it stands and falls with its content, that is, with the buildings that fill in the checkerboard. In general it liberates the city from the fetters of static social order and certainly expresses opportunity.

I understand that the American city cannot be described in terms of traditional urban spaces and monuments. Buildings serving special functions are of course present and may even have an imposing appearance. Since they are absorbed by the uniform urban pattern, however, they do not stand forth as in European cities. Quoting Benjamin Franklin's *Autobiography*, John Stilgoe points out that Franklin, arriving in Philadelphia in 1721, comprehended the particular nature of the grid, and Stilgoe concludes that, "Philadelphia prospered without a center. Instead of focusing on the great square [planned by Penn] it focused on nodes of activity."[76] J. B. Jackson adds an observation on New York, writing, "New Yorkers, . . . unlike the inhabitants of other cities, they demanded monumental buildings not as symbols of civic status, . . . but simply as curiosities."[77] "Nodes of activity" and "curiosities," both terms suggest that the American city is experienced as an incessant series of happenings, as a never-resting process that engages and fascinates. Instead of "nodes of activity," we could also say "expressions of activity." In the American city, in fact, the achievements of man the workman are presented to us in their full range of expression, from the vulgar to the sublime, and the city becomes indeed a forum for the freedom of choice.

Choice, however, implies identification, unless it becomes a mere matter of consumption. Therefore the expressions of activity must stand forth as visual images that convey a sense of meaning. In other words, the open city needs architectural *quality* more than the traditional city. Quality here means that each building has a distinct personality, without however becoming a mere caprice. How, then, was the need for quality satisfied? A panoramic view of Washington Street in Boston as it was in 1855 shows a series of adjacent, individual buildings of approximately the same width and varying height.[78] On each building is indicated the activity it houses and the name of the owner. The architecture is quite conventional and rather uniform, but a few inventions point in the direction of a more personal expression. In general the buildings have a dignified appearance and convey a sense of quality. A similar view of Chestnut Street in Philadelphia, c. 1879, shows a significant development. Each unit now has a distinct personality in terms of architectural form. Yet they still belong to the same family as a result of the general horizontal rhythm and the vertical superimposition of stories. The street front demonstrates that opportunity is a function of the open pattern and does not consist in a radical break with it. The street says, in a manner: "You all had the same chance, and you may demonstrate your success by getting up in the high, but you cannot step out of the system, because then freedom would turn into its opposite and become a destructive mutual fight."

Residential areas in American cities show an analogous relationship between the overall pattern and the individual unit. This is illustrated in a particularly fascinating way by the "painted ladies" of San Francisco; the wooden houses of the Victorian period that line the streets of the hilly city. Here, basically simple, boxlike volumes are dressed up with splendid facades in various styles: Italianate, Queen Anne, and San Francisco Stick.[79] Approximately sixteen thousand of these houses still stand, making the city a unique expression of the American dream. The authors of *Painted Ladies* cite a *New York Times* writer who visited San Francisco in 1883: "Nobody seems to think of building a sober house. Of all the efflorescent, floriated bulbousness and flamboyant craziness that ever decorated a city, I think San Francisco may carry off the prize. And yet, such is the glittering and metallic brightness of the air, when it is not surcharged with fog, that I am not sure but this riotous run of architectural fancy is just what the city needs to redeem its otherwise hard nakedness."[80] They are the result of an adaptation to local conditions, but the San Francisco houses are still eminently American in their individual expression within a continuous abstract grid. The pattern consisted of 25-foot-wide lots, and the

31

32

33

31.
Washington Street, Boston, MA, c. 1855.
32.
Chestnut Street, Philadelphia, PA, c. 1879.
33.
San Francisco, "painted ladies."

elaborate facades had to be made within narrow limits. A victory of the demand for quality resulted, as well as a most valuable source of information about the nature of the language of architecture. The title of a major study on the San Francisco houses is *A Gift to the Street*, a well-chosen one that suggests that a piece of good architecture makes the life of everybody richer, in particular when the open street is the forum where life takes place.[81]

The Back Bay in Boston is another major example of the American residential district. The area was filled in from c. 1858 on, and about thirty years later the main street, Commonwealth Avenue, was completed.[82] With its wide green in the middle and rows of distinguished, individual houses, it is perhaps the most splendid example of the open, American street that originated in Williamsburg. In Boston, however, it does not connect any "goals." The whole Back Bay is exclusively intended in terms of streets and series of lots; other buildings, such as churches, present within the area are in fact absorbed by the pattern. The houses lining the streets are all individual expressions, which, due to the unifying effect of rhythm and scale and the use of brick and brownstone, become members of the same family. The general quality is exceptionally high, even in comparison with any Old World street, and combines American openness with a sense of achievement and success.

These examples show that the built fabric of the American city represents a development of the original form of an open street lined by rows of separate, often symmetrical houses. This pattern has remained basic until today, even when the units have become skyscrapers. The American house was the point of departure with its representative front and more informal back. This proves the essentially democratic origin of the open city as an expression of the rights and opportunity of the individual. At the same time, however, the *typological* nature of the scheme has never ceased to be evident. The nineteenth-century settlements in the west prove this, with their rows of false shop and saloon fronts. In every city of the United States, thus, we spontaneously recognize that we are in America, rather than Europe or Asia.

During the process of urbanization, the American house underwent certain modifications. Urbanization means two things here: first, the formal problem of togetherness within the grid pattern, and second, the functional problem of work resulting from the change from a domestic to a commercial environment. The modifications mainly consisted in a relative loss of

34

35

34.
Back Bay, Boston.
35.
Dallas, c. 1980.

independence in favor of a repetitive pattern within which the individual building stands forth as a variation on common themes. This development was favored by the pronounced frontality of the modern house and was made possible by certain structural innovations. These innovations also allowed the incredibly fast urban expansion to occur that resulted from immigration, industrialization, and railroads.

The first innovation to be mentioned is the balloon frame. The traditional English wood frame, with mortise and tenon joints and clapboard siding, did not permit much variety in the articulation of the facades. When the machine-made nail appeared in the 1830's, it made a light and flexible skeleton possible, consisting of standard pieces of milled lumber. This balloon frame was used for the first time in a small Chicago church in 1839.[83] It soon revolutionized the building of wooden houses and led to a new architectural richness, as exemplified by the San Francisco facades. A large industry of prefabricated portable houses also came into being, especially in Chicago, and throughout the Great Plains the appearance of new towns was marked by its products.[84]

A few years after the balloon frame was introduced, the New York inventor James Bogardus started to use cast iron for the facades of urban buildings.[85] His first work, the Laing Stores of 1848, was a modular four-story building with facades consisting of regularly spaced iron columns: Corinthian on the ground floor and Tuscan above. The areas between the columns were entirely filled in by large windows over low parapets on the two upper floors. To express the continuity of the system, it also wrapped around the curved corner. The result was an extraordinarily rational building, as was Bogardus's own factory from 1849 where the treatment of the walls was even more uniform. Both buildings express better than any earlier structures the symbolic openness of the American grid. For the first time, American space had got an adequate architectural interpretation. I might add that Bogardus's buildings were the first true specimens of "pre-modern" architecture. His interpretation is not a fixed architectural form but rather, an open system like the grid itself, waiting to be occupied by individual expressions of activity. In his later works, Bogardus exploited the possibilities of expression by means of historical memories.

An analogous pursuit was carried out by his rival Daniel D. Badger, whose work is known because of the 1865 catalogue of his *Architectural Iron Works*.[86] Badger's sources of inspiration were many, but the

36

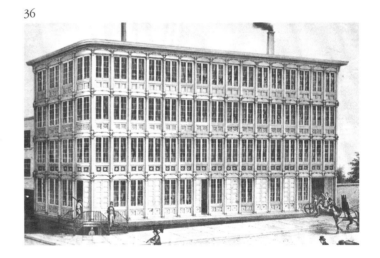

36.
Bogardus Factory, New York City, 1849.

33

37.
Haughwout Building, New York City, John P. Gaynor, 1856.
38.
SoHo, New York City.

Italian Renaissance *palazzo* served as a primary model for his facades of superimposed orders. The Venetian variety was particularly popular, probably because it combines a rich and picturesque appearance with lightness and transparency. In the introduction to his catalogue, Badger stresses "the superiority of the 'Badger fronts' in all buildings where large and attractive show windows were desirable . . . ," and he adds that: "Iron is capable of all forms of *architectural beauty.* It must be evident that whatever architectural forms can be carved or wrought in wood or stone, or other materials, can also be faithfully reproduced in iron." The iron front thus combines two aims: openness and beauty. Openness is a modern quality, while beauty is a result of historical memories, that is, of endowing the rational structure with motifs possessing figural quality and conventional meaning.

It would be too easy to reject the latter aim as a wish for a "cultural alibi."[87] It is certainly true that Badger and the other iron manufacturers did everything they could to make the facades look as if they were made of stone.[88] And still they are different from real stone buildings. Their lightness, sharp outlines, and transparent ground floors communicate a different character. Some might experience this as a disturbing contradiction, but the fact is that a new architectural idiom had been created that satisfied the American wish for expressions of activity. The regular structure and open walls of the iron-front "palaces" are, in fact, a manifestation of man the Workman rather than man the Aristocratic dweller. But why, then, were the motifs of Renaissance *palazzi* used? Evidently they were taken over to endow man's work with a sense of dignity and to mark the achievement of the individual. It is tempting to compare them with certain vernacular storehouses of the European past, where farmers kept the results of their toil: food, clothes, and precious things and accordingly transformed a basically simple building into an articulate "treasury."[89]

Iron fronts gave the American streetscape a varied order that also expressed the freedom and coherence of the grid. The method proved very successful, and series of iron buildings were erected in numerous American cities.[90] Today they have mostly disappeared, except in New York where there are close to 300 iron fronts, most concentrated in the SoHo district. We can still experience this major manifestation of the American city here and realize that an open form also makes human identification possible. The ongoing rehabilitation of many of the SoHo buildings is not just an expression of nostalgia; it also proves the capacity for change of this kind of architecture.

The iron front, however, could not cope with the need for larger dimensions that came forth toward the end of the nineteenth century, namely in Chicago after the great fire of 1871. Here a third technical innovation was necessary to permit a quick reconstruction of the destroyed downtown. After a first period of conventional building, William Le Baron Jenney erected the Home Insurance Building in 1884, the world's first building to use steel framing.[91] The new "Chicago construction" made possible structures of almost any height and at the same time liberated interior space from thick and inflexible load-bearing walls. The facade became a curtain that allowed for large areas of glass and a new freedom of articulation. The exterior of the Home Insurance Building, however, did not represent any innovation. It consisted of ten superimposed stories of stone and brick, united in groups of two or three by colossal classical pilasters. The difficult problem of articulating a building of this size is evident, and the classical language that had been developed to cope with bodies of a human scale did not offer any satisfactory solution. In 1879 Jenney himself had used a simpler approach in the first Leiter Building by superimposing a series of almost identical stories. In his second Leiter Building (1889–91), however, he arrived at a more promising scheme. In this building, the ground floor and a mezzanine are set off as a base for seven stories tied together by colossal classic pilasters. Between pilasters, the stories are subdivided in groups of three, two, and one by means of secondary orders of round Romanesque-looking shafts. The articulation of the top stories is ambiguous, and a sophisticated termination toward the sky is achieved. The second Leiter Building, now the Sears Store, is of immense size; yet still introduces movement and variety into the streetscape, thanks to its successful rhythmic articulation.

Jenney's achievement was of decisive importance, and his office also served as a training ground for several architects of the Chicago School, among them Louis Sullivan. In 1873 Sullivan came to Chicago from Boston via Philadelphia, where he had worked with Frank Furness. In his autobiography, Sullivan gives a famous description of his arrival by train; one that indeed reflects the open American world of the times. "Soon Louis caught glimpses of a great lake, spreading also like a floor to the far horizon, superbly beautiful in color, under a lucent sky. Here again was power, naked power, naked as the prairies, greater than the mountains. And over all spanned the dome of the sky, resting on the rim of the horizon far away on all sides, eternally calm overhead, holding an atmosphere pellucid and serene. And here again was a

39.
Second Leiter Building, Chicago, IL, William Le Baron Jenney, 1889–91.
40.
Schlesinger & Mayer Department Store (now Carson Pirie Scott and Co.), Chicago, IL, Louis H. Sullivan, 1898–1903.

40

41.
*Wainwright Building, St. Louis,
MO, Adler and Sullivan,
1890–91.*
42.
*Gage Building, Chicago, IL,
Louis H. Sullivan (facade),
1898–99.*

power, a vast open power, a power greater than the tiny mountains. Here, in full view, was the light of the world, companion of the earth, a power greater than the lake and the prairie below, but not greater than man in his power: So Louis thought. The train neared the city; it broke into the city; it plowed its way through miles of shanties disheartening and dirty gray. It reached its terminal at an open shed. Louis tramped the platform, stopped, looked toward the city, ruins around him; looked at the sky; and as one alone, stamped his foot, raised his hand and cried in full voice: *This is the Place for Me!* "[92]

Here any Puritan restraint is gone, and man has become free to carry on Jefferson's belief in the opportunities of the New World. But the dimension is different; the world has been liberated from any limit, and a new dynamism characterizes man's approach. We understand, however, that Sullivan was anything but blind to the values of nature. It is well known that "He was most at home in his rose gardens and happiest when drawing ornament."[93] Sullivan's dream was to bring meaning and beauty into the new environment. "If there are to be dreams, there must be dreamers to dream them—and there can be no greatness unless dreamers dream of it!" he said.[94] And then he asked his question about the tall office building: "How shall we impart to this sterile pile, this crude, harsh, brutal agglomeration, this stark, staring exclamation of eternal strife, the graciousness of those higher forms of sensibility and culture that rest on the lower and fiercer passions? How shall we proclaim from the dizzy height of this strange, weird, modern housetop the peaceful evangel of sentiment, of beauty, the cult of a higher life?"[95] Sullivan's answer was the Wainwright Building in St. Louis (1890–91), the Guaranty Building in Buffalo (1894–95), and the Bayard Building in New York (1897–98). Although none of these were erected in Chicago, they are the masterpieces of the style that, during the two decades about the turn of the century, gave Chicago one of the most impressive and unified cityscapes in the world.[96] What the iron fronts achieved at a smaller scale in New York, Chicago construction did to make skyscrapers become a new and more powerful expression of the concept of nodes of activity. Sullivan's contribution, however, was not only the masterpieces of the period but the first theory of the highrise. He realized that a very tall building also has to relate to earth and sky; it has to stand on the ground with "a great freedom of access" and terminate toward the sky. Inbetween is the world of man the Workman, "an indefinite number of stories of offices piled tier upon tier, one tier just like another tier, one office just like all the other offices . . . ."[97] Sullivan envisages a new *vertical* openness; man's achievement is not only expressed by a distinguished street front but also by the height of the building. Urban freedom has become total but remains *within the grid*, respecting the symbol of equal opportunity. And that, in fact, determines the power of Chicago's cityscape: the individual structure that stands and rises within the grid. In the past, standing was primarily a Classical quality and rising a Gothic one. Sullivan's buildings present both qualities but without any direct stylistic reference. Rather he returned to the "beginnings," reviving the basic properties of architectural form and letting them blossom in his incomparably beautiful ornament.

The buildings of Chicago are not only a manifestation of the open street; they also offer a new interpretation of the "nodes of activity" as such. I have in mind the spacious lobbies that receive the visitor and serve as a place of encounter. The first important example is the light court in the Rookery by Burnham and Root (1886–87). Here space expresses arrival and departure, encounter and movement, and enclosure and openness by means of flights of stairs, galleries, and the all-embracing skylight over an elegant iron construction. Today places of this kind within the grid have gained new actuality, indicating the need for what I have called islands of meaning.

With the rise of the skyscraper the American city changed, without, however, losing its basic identity. The change was experienced with particular intensity in New York, where the immigrants' first image of the New World was the cluster of large, highrise buildings in downtown Manhattan. Standing together in a dense cluster, these buildings seem to express arrival and prepare for the grid further up where the characteristic pattern of individual success becomes manifest. Many of the New York skyscrapers are based on a new interpretation of the vertical tripartite composition proposed by Sullivan and, with their articulated bases and fantastic tops, create the most exciting streetscape and skyline in the world. Let me just recall the Woolworth Building by Cass Gilbert (1911–1913) and the Chrysler Building by William Van Alen (1930). The Chrysler, in particular, has become one of the city's best-remembered landmarks thanks to its distinct image quality. It shows us how architecture may assure human orientation and identification in the open city. Although Manhattan is an island, it is experienced as an open form. The streets between Hudson River and East River do not lead to any goal but are suddenly cut off by the edge of the rivers, while the avenues seem infinite.

43.
Rookery, Chicago, IL, Burnham and Root, 1886–87.
44.
Manhattan.
45.
Chrysler Building, New York City, William Van Alen, 1930.

46.
*Central Park, New York City,
Frederick Law Olmsted and
Calvert Vaux, 1858–73.*
47.
*Rockefeller Center, New York
City, Associated Architects
(Todd, Robertson & Todd,
Reinhard & Hofmeister, Harvey
Wiley Corbett, Raymond
Hood), 1931–40.*

The idea of the grid as container of everything, including nature, also becomes manifest in Central Park, where Frederick Law Olmsted and Calvert Vaux created another kind of island of meaning. J.B. Jackson aptly calls the park "the democratic equivalent to the royal gardens and parks of Europe."[98] The development of the American city before World War II culminated with Rockefeller Center by a team of architects including Raymond Hood (1931–40). "Here almost everything that a city—or at least New York—should be comes together; skyscrapers, plazas, movement, detail, views, stores, cafés," Paul Goldberger writes. "It is all of a piece, yet it is able to appear possessed of infinite variety at the same time."[99] It is all of a piece because Rockefeller Center respects the grid and the street at the same time as it employs certain ideas of modern architecture to activate the space within the block. That is, the block is decomposed into a juxtaposition of slab-like buildings that correspond to the free-standing planes of Frank Lloyd Wright's houses. Thus the idea of the free plan is transferred to the scale of the city, and the general, modern concept of openness finds a particular American interpretation, as an island of meaning within the indeterminate grid.

My sketch of the nature and history of the American city has shown that it represents a valid alternative to the traditional European city. It also suggests that it satisfies basic needs of the open world. Unfortunately the lesson of the American city was not understood by the European pioneers of the Modern Movement. Le Corbusier's criticism of New York is well known, and Walter Gropius's studies for a new town with 30,000 inhabitants in Massachussets and for the development of Chicago South (1951–53) are based on the European concept of the "green city" rather than the American tradition.[100] The same holds true for Mies van der Rohe's Lafayette Park in Detroit (1955–63); his Illinois Institute of Technology in Chicago (begun 1939), however, represents an interpretation of the American campus ideal. The urban structures of Mies are certainly dignified, and the Seagram Building (1954–58) well partakes in the cityscape, as does the Chicago Federal Center (1959–64). Mies's architectural idiom furthermore represents a continuation of the Chicago tradition. His buildings lack, however, the capacity of variation that distinguished the iron fronts and Chicago construction. When buildings of his kind became numerous, a sterile and monotonous cityscape resulted, and the street lost its traditional value as a series of expressions of activity. Europeans often criticize Americans for not respecting their architectural heritage, but the American process of gradual change has certainly done less damage than the urban renewal of the 1960's inspired by European Modernism.

The disintegration of the city that took place during the 1960's and '70's has brought about reactions that aim at a recovery of true urban values. Kevin Lynch's analysis of urban structure in *The Image of the City* brought the problem to our attention, and his theory is certainly a useful tool for analysis of cities of any kind.[101] Although his empirical material is American, he does not do full justice to the problem of open form and, in particular, the open street. His understanding of urban structure, in fact, remains somewhat conventional, and he moreover leaves out its relationship to the concrete, built fabric. In spite of these shortcomings, Lynch's work represents an important contribution to our understanding of the city.

The decisive step toward the recovery of the idea of the city within the American tradition was taken by Robert Venturi, Denise Scott Brown, and Steven Izenour in *Learning from Las Vegas* (1972). In this work, the constituent role of the street is understood, and its actual manifestation as commercial strip is taken as a point of departure. The strip is first of all a function of the automobile, and accordingly the authors point out that its "supermarket windows contain no merchandise. There may be signs announcing the day's bargains, but they are to be read by pedestrians approaching from the parking lot. The building itself is set back from the highway and half hidden . . . [it] is low because air conditioning demands low spaces, and merchandizing techniques discourage second floors; its architecture is neutral because it can hardly be seen from the road."[102] What, then, is the role of the strip? "The zone *of* the highway is a shared order. The zone *off* the highway is an individual order. The elements of the highway are civic. The buildings and signs are private . . . . The system of the highway gives order to the sensitive functions of exit and entrance, as well as to the image of the strip as a sequential whole. It also generates places for individual enterprises to grow and controls the general direction of that growth. It allows variety and change along its sides and accommodates the contrapuntal, competitive order of the individual enterprises."[103] Could there be a better description of the American street in the age of the automobile than these lines? What, then, are the architectural consequences of the strip? Surprisingly, or perhaps not, they are exactly those properties I singled out as the constituent facts of the American street: "false" fronts with a distinct image quality in contrast with a less-pronounced back and "in-

48.
AT&T Building, New York City, Philip Johnson and John Burgee, 1979–84.
49.
Humana Tower, Louisville, KY, Michael Graves, 1982–85.

terior oases" that correspond to what we have called islands of meaning. The desired image quality is mainly achieved by understanding the building as a decorated shelter. This, however, is a question discussed in the third part of this study.

In downtown areas with a large number of highrise buildings, the problem of urban quality cannot be fully understood in "Las Vegas" terms. The street is not only for cars but in a conventional sense, for pedestrians as well. The sheer size of the structures puts the problem of "front" in a different light. Finally, the dense togetherness of the units demand a new interpretation of the rhythmical continuity found in New York's SoHo and Chicago's Loop districts. Many promising attempts have been made to recover the figural quality of downtown architecture in accordance with the new super dimensions. In general we may single out two endeavors: first, the wish to give each building a distinct figural quality and second, a more original approach to building consisting of a different adaptation of the highrise to the ground and sky.

The former aim found its first great manifestation in Philip Johnson and John Burgee's AT&T Building on Madison Avenue in New York (1979–84). Here Sullivan's tri-partite form is back but as a post-modern edition with base inspired by the Roman triumphal arch and top by the Baroque broken gable. The result is convincing; the building really possesses figural quality and stands out as a landmark among the many characterless late-modern slabs in Manhattan at the same time as the giant porch on the ground is a true gift to the street. The AT&T building inspired innumerable attempts at designing new tops. Interesting in this context was the 1983 design competition "Tops" sponsored by the Chicago Architectural Club.[104]

Michael Graves's Portland Building in Portland, Oregon (1980–82) and Humana Building in Louisville (1982–85) also represent the demand for figural quality. The means are more complex here, however, and comprise various historical memories as well as local references. After the competition for the Humana Building, the client wrote: "our desire was for the participants to focus on this particular context: the nineteenth-century architecture, the mixture of other buildings in the immediate area, its imposing geographic prominence in the city, and, most important, the Ohio River—where the city's life began. We further desired that the building enhance the overall visual impression of the Louisville skyline. These criteria are met in an extraordinary way by Michael Graves."[105] Graves achieved a similarly successful interpretation of place and task in Portland thanks to the image quality of his figurative composition. I will discuss his linguistic means in the third part of this study.

The second approach to the problem of the highrise is represented by Kohn Pedersen Fox, who in numerous projects have split the tower into a relatively low base of stone or other local material that adapts to the scale and character of the given environment and a high shaft, preferably of glass, that makes the volume dissolve toward the sky. The idea is certainly important and may often be a key to the recovery of urban values. It is related to the possibility of making new superbuildings appear as a neutral, reflecting background to smaller, but articulated, structures of more substantial materials, possibly civic institutions, such as churches, libraries, and city halls. In general the need for a cityscape that allows for orientation and identification is today fully realized.

The history of the American city is illuminating and significant: significant because it extends our understanding of the nature of man's urban environment in an open world and illuminating because it inspires our concrete design work. Summing up, I may say that the lessons offered by the American city are the demonstration that the identity of place can be combined with change and growth and that orientation and identification in the open city depend on architectural quality. The American identity of place does not consist in a traditional system of urban spaces and permanent landmarks, however, but rather, in a pattern capable of continuous transformations without losing its quality. Chicago offers the best illustration of this concept and also shows that the *genius loci*, as described by Sullivan, may be expressed convincingly in this way. Although all American cities are "American," each possess a distinct personality. Lewis Mumford's criticism of the grid as having "no order" is therefore untenable, and the experience of getting nowhere in the American city is a result of its openness.

The openness of the American city, however, is not something radically new. Rather it consists in a return to the beginnings, taking the street, the first human manifestation, as its point of departure. The American city is based on an archetype, but it does not accept any particular, historical interpretation of this type. Still, it includes the historical dimension through the language used by the architects to give concrete presence to the open pattern. When the grid is taken into possession by buildings that are expressions of activity, the American city shows what urban life means in the New World.

50

51

52

50.
333 Wacker Drive, Chicago, IL, Kohn Pedersen Fox, 1979–83.
51.
Pennsylvania Avenue, Washington, D.C.
52.
Flatiron Building, New York City, D.H. Burnham and Co., 1902.

The Language

In the introduction to his monograph *Buildings and Projects 1981–1986*, Robert A.M. Stern writes: "Architecture is less an issue of innovation than an act of interpretation; to be an architect is to possess an individual voice speaking a generally understood language of form." He continues: "Architecture is not a form of autobiography; it is not a lonely process of self-revelation. Architecture is a public act—a commemorative celebration of place and of culture. Yet architecture is not merely a kind of constructed evidence of events that happen in the culture as a whole . . . architecture has its own inner clock. Despite the chaos that rages everywhere around us, each building still presents an opportunity to affirm and reestablish the inherent order of things."[106]

Stern makes three assertions: that things possess an "inherent order," that architecture "interprets" this order in relation to the here and the now, and that this is done by means of a "generally understood language of form." Although written as an answer to the problems of today, Stern's conception of architecture is not new. It is in fact quite similar to that of Jefferson, who indeed dedicated much of his time to the study of the order of nature, and who wanted to use the "first principles of the art" to interpret his time and his place. When Stern repeats this traditional view, he evidently launches a protest against the modernist aim of "reinventing architecture from zero." Thus Giedion said, "Contemporary architecture . . . had to reconquer the most primitive things, as if nothing had ever been done before."[107] It is not clear, however, what Giedion meant by this statement. Two interpretations are possible. One corresponds to the functionalist creed that one should always start from zero, that is, from functions rather than architectural forms. The other, on the contrary, notices the aim of "reconquering the most primitive things," an idea similar to Kahn's concept of "beginnings." This was evidently what Le Corbusier had in mind when he formulated his "Five Points to a New Architecture."[108] The question is if such a reconquest can happen as if nothing had ever been done before. Does it not seem more reasonable to look for what is primitive or original in what *has* been done before?! Throughout its entire history, architecture has in fact rejected what was already there. In other words, forms do not lose their meaning when they are transferred in space and time. They are certainly subject to choice, and perhaps they may be devalued, but they do not become meaningless. If that were the case, American architecture from Jefferson on would have been senseless. My task, then, is to look at the history of American architecture to find out whether Jefferson's approach is still valid

53.
Old Ship Meetinghouse, Hing-
ham, MA 1681 (incorporating
1731 and 1755 additions).
54.
Old South Meetinghouse,
Boston, MA, 1729.

and to explain what the terms "inherent order," "interpretation," and "language of form" really mean.

The history of the American house and the urban building reveals a strong wish for *typical* solutions and for recurrent forms and principles. Let us see whether this finding is confirmed by other kinds of examples.

The meetinghouse was the first public institution in the New World and was moreover a true American invention. As such, it is of particular interest in my context, and I must ask, "How does man proceed when he faces a previously unknown task?" The early meetinghouses strike us, first of all, as extremely neutral. They are simple, elementary volumes without any decoration or formal articulation, and their interiors do not offer any surprises. The very term "meetinghouse" suggests that it was not intended as a church, or in other words, it was not intended as a place where certain values are kept and revealed and that possesses a sacred character in contrast to profane surroundings. Following Calvin's teachings, the Puritans aimed at a complete demystification of the world and rejected any kind of visual symbols. The church became a meetinghouse where individuals come together, not to experience a meaningful goal, but to share the belief that God helps the one who helps himself. "God blesseth his trade" is in fact the ethos of the American self-made man.[109] As an expression of utilitarianism, the meetinghouse does not contain an altar, and the congregation is assembled rather than directed. Here men come together as individuals, each one alone, with his family, in a separate box. The American idea of the open road that leads nowhere is here expressed, and after the gathering, the individual returns to his lonely path, which in itself represents the meaning of his action.

Still, the meetinghouse has an architectural form. Even the idea of nothingness has to be expressed. A neutral, square box, such as the Old Ship Meetinghouse in Hingham, Massachusetts (1681) serves the purpose well. It has no directionality and acts as a center without imposing any particular meaning. It is common but at the same time leaves the individual free. When the box became elongated, as in the Old South Meetinghouse in Boston (1729), the entrance was placed in the middle of the long side to prevent any sense of goal-orientation. The very absence of architectural motifs is also expressive. When particular forms are avoided, it is obviously because they *are* meaningful. If they were not, it would not make any difference to include them. Thus the Puritan meetinghouse tells us that a language of architecture exists, a language that, however, has to be used with extreme caution not to lead man into temptation. During its further development, the meetinghouse came to include certain distinct architectural elements, namely the steeple and the entrance porch. Both are intended as signals of presence rather than symbols, and their classical detailing adds a slight reference to enlightened man.

The meetinghouse also answers my question about how man proceeds when facing an unknown task, confirming that the early settlers returned to archetypes to obtain an environment corresponding to their purposes. In other words, they did not start from zero but reinterpreted known forms. Finally, the meetinghouse tells us something about basic forms as such, that is, about the dimensions of the language of architecture.[110]

What, then, are these dimensions? First, a building presents itself to us as a total figure, due to its volumetric shape and composition. The simple, elementary volume is essential to the appearance of the meetinghouse, and the addition of a steeple does not contradict this typological quality. Second, a building possesses a certain spatial organization, which not only serves a practical purpose but also expresses a conception of man's orientation and action in the world. Third, a building is articulated and detailed in a way that makes man's understanding of and identification with the concrete qualities of the environment manifest. The first, or figural, quality corresponds to the *what*, that is, to the thing we recognize and remember, whereas the second and third dimensions are properties that express *how* the thing is understood. In the case of the meetinghouse, these properties make clear a particular conception of the world and man's role in it manifest, a conception that formed a point of departure for American civilization and that was never entirely forgotten. As a consequence, the architectural properties of the meetinghouse endured. Its interior, thus, with galleries on three sides of a well-lit square or rectangular space, became a basic type expressing better than any other the democratic origin of American society. Being of this type, it is appropriate that Faneuil Hall in Boston should become the country's "Cradle of Liberty."

In spite of its essential nature, or rather because of it, the meetinghouse represents a particular and rather narrow understanding of the world. Jefferson's thinking broadened and humanized this view. In his chapter on "Religious Freedom" in *Notes on Virginia*

55.
First Congregational Church, Old Bennington, VT, 1806.
56.
Faneuil Hall, Boston, MA, after 1805-06 renovation by Charles Bulfinch of design by John Smibert, 1740–42.

57.
Greek Revival style meeting-house or church built in Sturgridge, MA, in 1832 for the local congregation of Baptists. The building was later moved to the Fiskdale section of Sturbridge and, in 1947 it was given by the Baptist Association to Old Sturbridge Village, an outdoor living history museum in Sturbridge, MA.

58

59

58.
University of Virginia, Charlottesville, VA, Thomas Jefferson, 1817-26.
59.
University of Virginia.

(1784), a new liberal attitude comes forth: "The legitimate powers of government extend to such acts only as are injurious to others. But it does me no injury for my neighbor to say there are twenty gods, or no god." How, then, did he express his wider understanding of democracy in terms of architecture? Primarily by adopting the classical language. A potential Classicism was already implicit in the Puritan meeting-house, but it was not allowed to express itself openly since the intended demystification did not permit the translation into architecture of any natural or human qualities. We could also say that Puritan "freedom" was a freedom of action rather than of expression. In Jefferson's world expression is legitimized, albeit with a certain moderation. This moderation is, by the way, contained in the very concept of Classicism, as opposed to more Baroque uses of the classical language.

Our basic knowledge about the nature of the classical orders goes back to Vitruvius. In his *De architectura*, he refers to human characters and in particular, to masculine and feminine qualities.[111] Our understanding of these meanings has been significantly extended and deepened by Vincent Scully in his study on Greek architecture.[112] Scully teaches that the orders and refinements of the classical language stem from the need to grasp and express the general properties of nature and man, as well as their interrelations; that is, what Robert A.M. Stern calls the "inherent order of things." This is not accomplished by means of an arbitrarily chosen code but rather, by a system of iconic forms that have qualities in common with their denotation. Hence the classical language has existential roots and is generally understood. When Jefferson talked about English architecture as a "wretched style," he probably had in mind the fact that the classical forces were used as decorative rather than constituent elements. To us, the point is not whether Jefferson's judgment is correct or not, but that he wanted a return to "first principles," and that he found them in a constituent use of classical language. In so doing he founded a truly democratic architecture, which, being a commonly understood act, served as a "celebration of place and of culture," to quote Robert A.M. Stern again.

As a model for his Classicism, Jefferson took Roman rather than Greek architecture. The choice is natural. Like America, the Roman Empire was a pluralistic society and needed a language capable of variety and local adaptation. But Jefferson went beyond Roman versatility. In Roman architecture, the *system* is always of primary importance as an expression of political absolutism. Jefferson, however, wanted to make liberty

and openness manifest. Therefore he treated the classical orders with a new freedom at the same time as he deprived the architectural ensemble of any static focus. The University of Virginia well illustrates his ends and means.[113] The layout of the campus reflects the traditional American green as well as the English quadrangle, but the continuous colonnades that accompany the space are instead derived from the *fora* of Roman imperial architecture. Jefferson, however, avoided the uniformity of the model, introducing along either side of the colonnade five classical pavilions for professors. These pavilions appear as variations on a common theme, transferring the ensemble into an academic village consisting of individual personalities belonging to the same family. On axis, at the end of the lawn, Jefferson placed a Pantheon-like library that corresponds to the dominant temple of the Roman forum. The building, however, does not act as a goal but rather, as a point of departure. This interpretation is confirmed at the opposite open end of the campus, where the axis extends infinitely into the landscape.[114] A significant expression of the role of education in American democracy is here realized, as well as an eminently human environment.

To gain a better understanding of Jefferson's conception of architecture, it is necessary to add a few words about his Virginia Capitol in Richmond (1788). As is well known, the model was the so-called Maison Carrée in Nîmes. Here, too, the choice is natural, considering the open, axial organization of the Roman temple, which through its spacious porch dominates the land in front. Again, however, Jefferson humanizes the building, making it look more like a large house than a seat of power. Jefferson's deep sense of the characters of various building tasks is thereby confirmed, as is his mastery of the classical language. With the domestic world of Monticello, the democratic togetherness at the University, and the public order of the Capitol, Jefferson managed to translate the microcosmos in which he believed into architectural forms.

About the same time as Jefferson operated in the South, a different Classicism developed in New England. Here the source of inspiration was British architecture, in particular the works of the Adam brothers. In general this architecture was based on distinct, typological volumes, and the classical orders served as decoration rather than constituent elements. The result is somewhat cool and abstract in character, in contrast to the warm humanity of Jefferson's buildings. Evidently Puritan memories linger on, as does a general northern spirit. The approach is already present in

60.
Virginia State Capitol, Richmond, VA, Thomas Jefferson, 1788.
61.
First Congregational Church, Old Bennington, VT.

the MacPhaedris-Warner House in Portsmouth, New Hampshire (1718–23), and numerous other examples from the following decenniums could be cited.[115]

In Charles Bulfinch, northern Classicism found a worthy interpreter. His major work, the Massachusetts State House (1795–98), well illustrates his aims and his way of using the classical vocabulary. In general the building appears as an inventory of basic forms: the primary prismatic volume, the protecting arched porch and superposed colonnade, the pediment on pilasters above, and the crowning, elementary dome. The windows are cut into the brick wall without surrounds; only two Adamesque openings based on the *serliana* are introduced on the wings to give these a certain figural independence. A composition of volumes results, whose unsubstantial character has been pointed out by Pierson.[116] Compared with William Chambers's Somerset House in London (1776–86), which might have served as a source of inspiration, everything is in fact abstract and typical. An American sense of form is evident; for example, it determines the openness of the double-story porch. Bulfinch's quest for archetypal forms culminated with his Meetinghouse in Lancaster, Massachusetts (1816–17). Again we find a composition of elementary volumes and a restrained decoration by means of classical elements. The character is light and transparent. The steeple, conceived as an interesting synthesis of tower and dome, is crowned by a circular *tempietto*, a motif that in less-pronounced editions is quite common in American churches.[117] Probably it echoes the small cupola, which has been a token of American public buildings since Williamsburg. How, then, did Bulfinch employ the classical vocabulary? In contrast to the constituent role given to classical elements by Jefferson, Bulfinch used the classical language to articulate and characterize his volumes. He distinguished the different parts at the same time as he tied them together to form an integrated whole. Thus he demonstrated that architectural articulation consists in simultaneous separation and unification. In addition he gave each part an appropriate character. At Lancaster, for instance, the porch is Doric, whereas the crowning *tempietto* is Ionic. In general the classical elements are used as memories by Bulfinch, while Jefferson aimed at a true *revival* of the classical language. Jefferson gave a new interpretation of the southern world of basic, substantial characters; Bulfinch, on the contrary, worked with transferred forms, which, being exposed to a Nordic environment, had become subject to a certain dematerialization. Thus we find in America the distinction between north and south present in the Old World. This does not mean that we have two

62

62.
Massachusetts State House, Boston, MA, Charles Bulfinch, 1795-98.
63.
Lancaster meetinghouse, Lancaster, MA, Charles Bulfinch, 1816-17.

63

entirely different modes of expression. In both cases the classical language is the primary means of communication, and in both cases it is used in an American way.

At this point I return to the question as to whether forms change, or even lose, their meaning when they are transferred in space and time. The history of architecture in general, and the history of American architecture in particular, show that the basic meanings contained in the classical forms have been alive since antiquity and have constituted a generally understood language. The vitality of classical forms resides in their being expressions of timeless natural and human characters. It is wrong, therefore, to say that they belong to the past, or that their content is outdated. Because of its existential roots, it is also dubious whether the classical language may be superseded by a new idiom that possesses an analogous capacity of expression. Evidently, however, the meanings of the classical forms have to be conquered over and over again through local and temporal interpretations. "Language is the house of Being," Heidegger says,[118] and as a sub-language, the classical language of architecture houses basic modes of man's "being in space." The problem, therefore, is not whether classical forms may be used, but how they should be used. The architecture of Jefferson and Bulfinch represent two possible modes of use, but the possibilities are evidently legion. Let me just recall the architects of the European Renaissance and Baroque who, each in his own way, managed to interpret place and culture in relation to the inherent order of things. It is also important to note that Jefferson's and Bulfinch's works represent two different cases of Palladianism. The former adopted Palladio's use of the classical orders to humanize and characterize his buildings, while Bulfinch was inspired by the Italian master's way of composing with distinct, elementary units. These choices were possible because of the generality of Palladio's architecture; more than anyone else Palladio developed a variety of the classical language that seems to fit everywhere.[119]

But uses are also possible that imply a devaluation of the inherent meanings. Such a devaluation of symbols took place during the nineteenth century and led to a situation that demanded a general cleaning up. This is implicit in Giedion's words that architecture had to reconquer the most primitive things, as if nothing had ever been done before. The reason for the devaluation was, according to Giedion, the self-made man's need for a "cultural alibi."[120] Giedion traces this need back to Napoleon's will for power, but in my context

64

64.
North Grand Watertower, St. Louis, MO, George Barnett, 1871.

65.
Brooklyn Institute of Arts and Sciences (Brooklyn Museum), Brooklyn, NY, McKim, Mead and White, 1893ff.
66.
Woolworth Building, New York City, Cass Gilbert, 1911–13.

the American substitution of the "pursuit of happiness" with the "pursuit of gain" is a better explanation. Again classical forms were employed but this time to express mere material success. As a consequence, articulation and characterization gave way to a pompous exhibition of superficial effects. In buildings such as the Rhode Island State House in Providence (1891–1904) and the Brooklyn Institute of Arts and Sciences (1893ff.), both by McKim, Mead and White, all elements are treated as if they were of primary importance.[121] Hence they compete rather than support each other, which results in a pseudo-composition where shallow themes are played out *fortissimo*.

We must also, however, take a brief look at another mode of expression that is part of the history of American architecture. What I have in mind is the Gothic idiom, which arose with the Picturesque movement. The Gothic is also a consistent system of meaningful forms, and as such a language, it may be transferred and reinterpreted. The inherent content, however, is different from that of Classicism and constitutes a supplement rather than a substitute. Whereas classical forms express basic characters of nature and man, the Gothic takes a negation of these very characters as its point of departure, aiming at a general spiritualization that dematerializes the bodily substance of the architectural members. This implies that the Gothic idiom has a more special scope than the classical language, and that its capacity of expression is much more limited. Consequently, Gothic forms appear less general and do not impart the same sense of timelessness as the classical. I might also add that Gothic spiritualization does not suit American utilitarianism particularly well. The Gothic, in fact, remained a peripheral phenomenon in the history of American architecture, while the classical language served for two centuries as the primary means to make architecture an authentic part of the cultural identity of the country.

The profound change in outlook and aims that characterizes American post-Civil War society was felt already before the war and became manifest in architecture as a wish for self-expression. The Civil War accelerated this process, and since it caused the disintegration of traditional values and ways of life, it opened up a new dynamism and aggressiveness. In short, the melting pot, which had Jefferson's democratic microcosmos as its objective, was superceded by pluralistic diversity. Hence the fragmentation inherent in the American situation became total, and a world of separate bits resulted. I have already suggested that in architecture this state of affairs brought about a devaluation of symbols. The classical language was no longer capable of serving as a common means of understanding but had to become part of a more complex totality.

During the decades following the Civil War, the new situation induced talented architects to look for fresh ways of expression. The first who ought to be mentioned is Frank Furness, who more than any of his contemporaries attempted a radical new departure.[122] To a classically educated eye, the buildings of Furness may seem arbitrary, mannered, or even repulsive. Elements of the most diverse origin are gathered: medieval and classical, oriental and western, monumental and vernacular. Indeed an architecture of bits! But the parts are kept together by an exceptional sense of the "first principles of the art." Here these principles have not been distilled into an equilibrated classical code but appear in their original form as modes of standing, rising, opening, and closing and as expressions of hardness and softness, lightness and heaviness. Furness's compositions are also original, based on symmetry and asymmetry, separation and unification, additive superimposition and organic integration. His buildings, therefore, have to be read like a complex musical score, say a movement from a Mahler symphony, where themes, rhythms, and instruments mingle and interpenetrate. And still, Furness remains an American architect. His aim is openness, not in the former sense of freedom in space, but as a new openness of content, whereby the building is transformed into a *collage* of memories. These memories, however, are not of an autobiographical nature but rather, are contained in "Volume Zero" of history.

The aims of Furness's contemporary, Henry Hobson Richardson, were somewhat similar and yet quite different. Again we find a wish for returning to basic qualities, but rather than making them part of a complex collage, Richardson chose one distinct mode of expression known today as "Richardsonian Romanesque." Located in history between classical antiquity and the Gothic, the Romanesque possesses some qualities of both. It is solid and earthly, and at the same time it is the expression of a certain spiritualization. It has a synthetic character and satisfied the need of the period for a more comprehensive language. Richardson's handling of the idiom, however, is original and creative. No direct historical models for his buildings exist; rather they are solutions to modern building tasks. This is particularly evident in his masterpiece, the Marshall Field Wholesale Store in Chicago (1885–87, demolished 1930). The basic qualities of standing, rising, opening, and closing are expressed

67.
Pennsylvania Academy of the Fine Arts, Philadelphia, PA, Frank Furness, 1871–76.
68.
Marshall Field Wholesale Store, Chicago, IL, Henry Hobson Richardson, 1885–87.

69.
Guaranty Building, Buffalo, NY, Adler and Sullivan, 1894–95.
70.
Larkin Company Administration Building, Buffalo, New York, Frank Lloyd Wright, 1904.

in this building with a convincing simplicity of means, which prepared for the great achievements of the Chicago School. Richardson was born in the South, and although he chose Boston as his place of study and work, he remained a Southerner. This comes forth in his well-balanced compositions, his emphasis on substance, and his warmth of expression. The synthesis of romantic and classical qualities achieved by Richardson made a strong impact abroad. European architects visited the United States toward the end of the nineteenth century to study his works; for the first time American architecture had become a source of inspiration to the Old World.

Louis Sullivan also found his point of departure in Richardson's works, and even in his last buildings the characteristic Richardsonian arch appears. First, however, Sullivan aimed at finding his own answer to the demands of the epoch. We have already mentioned how he transformed the "crude, harsh and brutal pile" of the tall office building into an expression of "sensibility and culture" using a new interpretation of the basic qualities of standing and rising. This interpretation not only determines the overall tri-partite composition but is emphasized and explained by ornamentation. As convincingly demonstrated by Scully, Sullivan's ornament serves to make "the forces which move through all matter . . . humanly comprehensible through . . . empathy . . . ." And Scully concludes: "Because of its ornament, . . . the Guaranty Building becomes more than a simple skeleton of slender steel members and acts instead as a skeleton cladded with what appears to be integral force, stepping out toward its corner, standing, stretching, and physically potent."[123]

In the works of Furness, Richardson, and Sullivan, we encounter three different attempts at conquering the devaluation of symbols.[124] Being almost devoid of historical references, Sullivan's answer is the most modern, but today we understand that Furness's less perfected works may have more to tell us. Richardson's idiom is of minor actuality, but like no one else, he teaches us what figural quality, articulation, and detailing mean.

It was Frank Lloyd Wright, however, who with his destruction of the box managed to give American architecture a new start, which at the same time represented a continuation of the original aims of openness and democracy. I will not repeat what has already been said about Wright's grammar in connection with his houses but only ask if it really constitutes a language of architecture. Evidently, Wright's juxtaposition of vertical and horizontal planes satisfies only one of the dimensions mentioned in connection with the Puritan meetinghouse. It is a means of spatial organization and must be combined with figural elements and concrete detailing to form a language. Figural elements were always present in Wright's works, although less pronounced in his Usonian phase, possibly as a result of modernist influence. And he certainly always wanted to be "natural" in his use of materials.[125] Still, it cannot be denied that a certain lack of figural quality is felt. Wright's forms are only nameable things to a certain extent and are not, therefore, fully satisfying as a poetical tool. Or rather, the poetical value of his works is exceptionally high, but one-sided.

It is precisely a one-sidedness of this kind that distinguishes modernist architecture. Giving almost exclusive attention to *space*, the Modern Movement neglected the typological dimension and in general, the aim of creating concrete *places*. It may be objected that Le Corbusier's Five Points do represent an attempt to establish first principles, and that they are related to the qualities of standing, rising, and opening. But they do not constitute a language since they are principles rather than a set of nameable things. As a result of its abstract approach, modern architecture lost contact with man's daily life and produced a monotonous and sterile environment. It is the great paradox of modernism that it wanted to be open and inclusive and ended up being one-sided and exclusive. As a reaction, late modern architecture went through an expressionist phase during the '50's and '60's. Neo-expressionism, however, aimed at arbitrary effects rather than meaningful discourse and could not serve as a basis for any further development. Typical examples of this current are the City Halls in Boston and Dallas.[126]

During its entire history, architecture was never trapped in a more desperate impasse than the late modernism of the post-World War II period. In spite of single masterpieces such as Le Corbusier's church, Notre-Dame du Haut at Ronchamp (1950–55), and Mies van der Rohe's National Gallery in Berlin, (1962–67) the situation seemed hopeless. What had been a generally understood means of communication had degenerated into sterile functionalism on the one hand or arbitrary self-expression on the other.

Toward the end of the 1950's, however, Louis Kahn broke the spell by asking his famous question: "What does the building want to be?" To find his answer he returned to the "beginnings" and said: "What will be

71.
Kimbell Art Museum, Fort Worth, TX, Louis I. Kahn, 1969–72.

has always been." He went on: "Order is." "Order is the sum total of all the laws of nature." "Design is form-making in order." "Form is what." "Design is how." "Form comes from wonder." "Man lives to express." And as a conclusion, "A work of architecture is an offering to Architecture."[127] In these aphorisms a whole philosophy of architecture is contained. It says that our task is to express the inherent order of things, and that can only be done if we face the world with wonder. What we understand has to be set into work through design, and the result, the work of architecture, is an offering to Architecture with a capital "A". Architecture with a capital "A" is that part of our field that belongs in Volume Zero, that is, its beginnings or *language*. We recall Heidegger's dictum "Language is the House of Being" and realize the affinity between the thoughts of the two men.[128]

Kahn's ideas, however, would not have had the same impact if he had not demonstrated their validity in his works. Here, finally, we encounter in our time a complete approach that comprises the typological dimension, as well as the organization of space and formal articulation. Vincent Scully had already recognized the importance of Kahn's achievement in 1962 and wrote, "The impression becomes inescapable that in Kahn, as once in Wright, architecture began anew."[129] The fact that it began anew, however, is also the shortcoming of Kahn's architecture. Although his buildings necessarily are circumstantial interpretations of what is general, they seem strangely timeless and somehow remote from the complexities and contradictions of present society. They do not really express the open world of bits, but they certainly tell us that we need a return to things themselves.

The wish to include the "richness and ambiguity of modern experience" was the point of departure for Robert Venturi,[130] and thereby he transformed Kahn's "order is" into the "difficult whole." It might seem paradoxical that Venturi used history to approach modern experience, but in so doing he recognized that man's identity consists of memories. "As an architect I try to be guided not by habit but by a conscious sense of the past," he writes and quoting T.S. Eliot, continues, "Tradition . . . cannot be inherited, and if you want it you must obtain it by great labor."[131] The result of Venturi's great labor was his book *Complexity and Contradiction in Architecture*, in which he systematically presents the problems of architectural form as they become evident in major works from the past and present. In explicit opposition to the Modern Movement, Venturi succeeded in reconquering not-so primitive things by looking carefully at what had been done before.[132]

Venturi also illustrated his theory with appropriate projects, where bits of past and present experience are brought together in collage-like compositions that, in spite of their complex content, also possess a convincing figural duality. His Carll Tucker III House in Westchester County, N.Y. (1975) illustrates the point. Here a distinct form is simultaneously "house," "garden pavilion," "tower," and "balcony on the world."[133]

Venturi's language is a language of memories, where beginnings, past and present, unite to make the beholder feel more alive in a profound and meaningful sense. In his later writings, he has himself defined his method as the making of a "shelter with decoration on it."[134] In my terminology "shelter" may be translated into "general figural quality," while "decoration" stands for "articulation," and "detailing" for particular images. Moreover shelter takes care of functional needs, whereas decoration, to cite Venturi's own words, satisfies the "expressive wants of many different people." Venturi's concept of decoration seems without limits; in a project for a Jazz Club in Houston (1978), it even embraces a full-rigged sailing ship placed on top of the roof. We might infer from this that Venturi's interpretation of a building task is radically new. At the same time, however, it is also old, and in fact, his aim is an inclusive architecture consisting of "conventional elements used in a new context."[135]

In the work of Michael Graves, we find a similar and different approach to the problem of language. Whereas Venturi is always different, Graves's aim is to develop a systematic vocabulary that may be used in connection with any building task. We could also say that language is more important to him than the complexities of the circumstantial situation. However, his vocabulary has proved capable of adaptation to functions ranging from houses to high-rise buildings and to environments as different as New Jersey and Southern California. What is common to Venturi and Graves is the historical basis; Graves's forms are clearly derived from the past, but as a rule they have undergone a process of stylization whereby an idiom that is new as well as old results.

Graves himself has given a kind of inventory of his vocabulary in a drawing that opens a book on his work.[136] It is called *Rome 1981*, and the title, as well as the representation itself, shows that the architecture of ancient Rome is his main source of inspiration. In

72.
Carll Tucker III House, Westchester Co, NY, Robert Venturi, 1975.
73.
Rome 1981, *Michael Graves.*

contrast to Jefferson, however, Graves is not particularly interested in the classical orders but rather, in the figural motifs of monumental and vernacular buildings. The text that accompanies the drawing is in fact called "A Case for Figurative Architecture" and represents a return to an understanding of architecture as an expression of natural and human characters. And the means to reach this goal is a language of distinct architectural elements.

Michael Graves's development illustrates the present situation. His first works were still designed in the late-modern mode, transforming the building into an equilibristic tri-dimensional collage of abstract elements (Hanselmann House, 1967; Benacerraf House, 1969; Snyderman House, 1972). Then followed a quest for figurative forms (Schulman House, 1976; Fargo-Moorhead Cultural Center Bridge, 1977), and finally he arrived at a fully developed language, which found its first convincing manifestation in the Plocek House in Warren, New Jersey (1977). The Portland Building (1980–82) proves the validity of Graves's mature style. Known architectural elements are modified and combined in a fascinating way in this building. The horizontally extended base with its loggia is related to the surrounding streets as it supports the enclosed block above. This primary volume has solid corners and small, widely spaced windows. The simple figure, however, is interpenetrated by a grand, symbolic portal motif, formed by two immense, fluted "pilasters," which also recall the vertical ribs of conventional skyscrapers. Over the "pilasters" two giant brackets hold up an equally colossal "keystone," which is subdivided by modern strip windows. The fan-like shape and shiny surface of the keystone relates the building to the sky and prepares for the concluding "head," which, unfortunately, has not been finished according to Graves's design. It is an ingenious interpretation of the classical tripartite composition, indeed, and an intriguing use of known elements! In general the Portland building combines the concept of open content with a powerful, figural form that expresses its civic meaning.

My discussion of Venturi's and Graves's work has shown that the problem of language is today understood. Thus the examples support Robert A.M. Stern's statement of aims, which was taken as my point of departure. In different but related ways the works of Venturi, Stern, and Graves represent a new eclecticism that serves the expressive wants of the open world. They are all exponents of a true American architecture. Their similarity resides in the search for what is typical, or, in the words of Stern, for

74

75

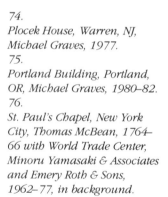

76

74.
*Plocek House, Warren, NJ,
Michael Graves, 1977.*
75.
*Portland Building, Portland,
OR, Michael Graves, 1980–82.*
76.
*St. Paul's Chapel, New York
City, Thomas McBean, 1764–
66 with World Trade Center,
Minoru Yamasaki & Associates
and Emery Roth & Sons,
1962–77, in background.*

"icons of permanence." Their differences show that a multiplicity of personal idioms may be developed on this common basis.

In general the history of the language of architecture in America proves that man does not proceed from zero when he is allowed a new start. Or rather, zero does not mean nothing but, in Kahn's sense, the beginnings. From the outset, American architecture implied a search for first principles or archetypes, and history was the necessary source of information. As such, first principles do not exist. Through their circumstantial manifestations, however, they may be understood, and a language of architecture may be derived from this understanding. Thus history teaches us how the here and the now can be interpreted through a generally understood language of form. In an open world of separate bits such a language is the only possible common denominator. Hence, American architecture initiates the New World Architecture we all need today.

Conclusion

One of the key concepts used in this study is openness, denoting the pluralistic condition that characterizes the modern world. In human terms, it ought to imply freedom of choice and equal opportunity. Evidently openness also implies a dissolution of the ethnic domains of the past and, as a result, a fragmentation of the world. My initial question was whether it is possible to gain a foothold in the open world, and as an answer, I suggested that openness requests a new interpretation of the three basic dimensions of architecture: *space, form,* and *type* or, in short, a new understanding of the language of architecture.

The American experience proves that pluralistic fragmentation does not impede the development of a generally understood language of architecture but, rather, demands its formation. Whereas in the past architecture served to visualize the particular "ethnic domain,"[137] it cannot now accomplish anything but the creation of "islands of meaning" within the encompassing openness. These islands are the result of a choice between qualities, but they ought to be realized by means of a common language that renders reciprocal communication possible. Such a language has to be existentially rooted as a manifestation of the inherent order of things. The dimensions of architecture, space, form, and type thus correspond to the human modes of being in the world, known as orientation, identification, and recognition (memory).

In the open world, the street is the archetypal *spatial* form, expressing man's orientation as a "being on the way." The street has in fact always been the constituent element of the American city. When it generates a grid pattern, general openness results, indicating the idea of equal opportunity. It would be mere nostalgia to advocate today more traditional urban structures inspired, for example, by Mediterranean villages. The opening up of the world is an irreversible process, and the city has to reflect this situation. Within the open city, however, the islands of meaning may exhibit a traditional pattern.[138]

In the individual building, the free plan is generally recognized as the modern answer to the demand for openness. Today we understand, however, that defined focuses and paths have to be introduced, for instance by means of central and axial symmetry, in order to make the free plan an expression of an accomplished choice. In general the history of American architecture comprises a realistic development of the free plan, from the destruction of the box by Frank Lloyd Wright to the articulate openness of Robert A.M. Stern.

Modern architecture intended openness almost exclusively in terms of space, whereas the built *form* was reduced to a juxtaposition of neutral, abstract elements. The reason was part of a wish to expunge all historical memories, as if newness consists in the illusion that nothing had ever been done before. American architecture, on the contrary, has always been concrete in character and has conceived the built form as an open composition of nameable parts. Thomas Jefferson understood that when he wanted to free American architecture from the "wretched style" of the English. At the same time, his quest for first principles shows that openness does not mean self-expression of arbitrary choice but rather, a new interpretation of known forms. With the disruption of the traditional ways of life following the Civil War, ideal openness developed into a more explicit openness of content.

In general the concrete approach characteristic of American architecture implies a pragmatic respect for man's everyday life. After a dangerous period of abstraction before and after World War II, Robert Venturi brought the things themselves back to our attention and opened up a new realism in architecture, taking man's identification with what is there as his point of departure. This identification is ultimately based on our sense of standing, rising, opening, and closing, and its object is a built form that expresses our mode of being in space.

The third aspect of the language of architecture, the *typological* dimension, is today at the center of our interest. At last we realize that our foothold is primarily a function of recognition. In an open world, this means that each building stands forth as a distinct something, possessing what I have called a "figural quality." This implies a return to archetypal beginnings, that is, to man's original recognition and naming of identities. Louis Sullivan's characterization of the "tall office building" and Frank Lloyd Wright's thoughts about the "natural house" illustrate this quest for identity. America, as an open society, has aimed from the very beginning at the development of commonly understood types.

Our only source of information about architectural types is history. History has in fact always been a major preoccupation of American architects, not because they needed a "cultural alibi," as suggested by Giedion,[139] but because they wanted to understand what architecture is all about. The use of the past as an exercise of freedom is called *eclecticism.* American architecture illustrates the eclectic nature of our field, as expressed in Louis Kahn's dictum, "What will be has always been." Kahn's words may seem strange in a world of change, but change necessarily implies that "something" changes. Our understanding of the language of architecture, however, ought to prevent eclecticism from degenerating into an arbitrary play with effects as so often happens today.

The history of American architecture has moreover shown that certain identities tend to reappear, in particular, classical forms. I have explained this fact as a result of their being an expression of basic existential structures. It is therefore not surprising that the classical forms are being revived today. I have also suggested that they become part of a more complex language. To illustrate this demand, I have followed the development of the architectural medium from Frank Furness to Michael Graves. When the Old World opens up, the particular local traditions should not disappear but, as expressions of the spirit of the place, become part of the new language.

Today we all stand alone without the support of an integrated and stable culture. To make this open condition meaningful, we must choose between qualities and understand our choice as an interpretation of the inherent order of things. Such an interpretation implies that an individual voice speaks a commonly understood language. Our primary task as architects, therefore, is to learn the language of architecture and to gain experience in its use. Our goal is the creation of a generally and locally meaningful New World Architecture. The American experience shall be our guide.

Notes

1) Especially after the Revolution (Declaration of Independence 1776).

2) Thomas Paine, "Common Sense," (1776) in Thomas Paine *Common Sense and Other Political Writings* (New York: Bobbs-Merrill Company, Inc., 1953).

3) Christian Norberg-Schulz, *Roots of Modern Architecture* (Tokyo, forthcoming).

4) László Moholy-Nagy, *Vision in Motion* (Chicago: Paul Theobald and Company, 1947).

5) Richard Saul Wurman, *What Will Be Has Always Been: The Words of Louis I. Kahn* (New York: Access Press Ltd. and Rizzoli, 1986), pp. 150ff.

6) Daniel J. Boorstin, *The Lost World of Thomas Jefferson* (1948; Boston: Beacon Press, 1960).

7) Max Weber, *Die protestantische Ethik* (München, 1969), p. 122.

8) "Quality" comes from Latin *qualis*: "of what kind."

9) Wurman, *What Will Be Has Always Been*, pp. 150ff.

10) Boorstin, *The Lost World*, p. 229.

11) Boorstin, *The Lost World*, p. 248. Also Weber, *Die protestantische Ethik*, p. 131.

12) Vincent J. Scully, Jr., *The Shingle Style* (1955; New Haven: Yale University Press, 1971), p. 162ff.

13) William H. Pierson, Jr., *American Buildings and Their Architects*,1, *The Colonial and Neoclassical Styles* (1970; New York: Anchor Press/ Doubleday, 1976).

14) Pierson, *American Buildings*, 1, pp. 24, 51.

15) Pierson, *American Buildings*, 1, pp. 31 etc.

16) M.W. Barley, *The English Farmhouse and Cottage* (London: Routledge and Kegan Paul, 1961).

17) In February 1704 a group of Indians and Frenchmen organized by Governor de Vaudreuil of Canada attacked Deerfield. They burned the town, killed 48 inhabitants and carried off 111 captives. Samuel Chamberlain, Henry N. Flynt, *Historic Deerfield: Houses and Interiors* (New York: Hastings House, 1972), pp. 8-9.

18) Pierson, *American Buildings*, 1, pp. 73ff.

19) *Mount Vernon: An Illustrated Handbook* (Mount Vernon: The Mount Vernon Ladies' Association of the Union, 1974), p. 42.

20) Rhys Isaac, *The Transformation of Virginia 1740–1790* (Chapel Hill: The University of North Carolina Press, 1982), p. 33.

21) Donald D. Friary, "The noncollectors: Henry and Helen Flynt and Historic Deerfield," *Antiques*, Vol. CXXI, no. 1 (January, 1982). Also, *Antiques*, Vol CXXVII, no. 3 (March, 1985). The entire issue is devoted to historic Deerfield.

22) Pierson, *American Buildings*, 1, pp. 142ff.

23) The porches at Shirley were added in 1831. Hugh Morrison, *Early American Architecture* (New York: Oxford University Press, 1952), p. 369.

24) Robert A.M. Stern, *Pride of Place* (New York: Houghton Mifflin Company, 1986), p. 1.

25) Pierson, *American Buildings*, 1, p. 291.

26) Thomas Jefferson, "Query XV, Colleges, Buildings, and Roads," *Notes on the State of Virginia* (1787) ed., William Peden (1954; New York: W.W. Norton & Company, 1972).

27) Thomas Jefferson, letter to Maria Cosway in William Howard Adams, *Jefferson's Monticello* (New York: Abbeville Press, 1983), pp. 44, 116.

28) Adams, *Jefferson's Monticello*, p. 192. The expression stems from Mario Praz.

29) Which is a "Roman" approach, as opposed to the plastic art of Greece.

30) Vincent J. Scully, Jr., *American Architecture and Urbanism* (New York: Praeger Publishers, Inc., 1969), p. 121.

31) Scully, *American Architecture*, p. 52.

32) Ralph Waldo Emerson, *Nature* (1836), Chapter I.

33) Emerson, *Nature*, Chapter III.

34) William H. Pierson, Jr., *American Buildings and their Architects*, 2, *Technology and the Picturesque* (New York: 1978; Anchor Press/Doubleday, 1986).

35) Pierson, *American Buildings*, 2, p. 354.

36) John W. Dietrichson, *The Image of Money* (Oslo: The American Institute Press at the Universty of Oslo, 1969), p. 371.

37) Stern, *Pride of Place*, pp. 85ff.

38) Scully, *The Shingle Style*.

39) Christian Norberg-Schulz, "The Swiss Style," in Werner Blaser, *Fantasy in Wood: Elements of Architecture at the Turn of the Century*, trans. C. Neuenschwander and D. Qu. Stephenson (Basel: Boston: Birkhauser Verlag, 1987).

40) Scully, *The Shingle Style*, p. 127.

41) Mariana Griswold Van Rensselaer, *Henry Hobson Richardson and His Works* (1888; New York: Dover Publications, Inc., 1969), p. 115.

42) John Jacob Glessner, "The Story of a House," (1923) in *The House at 1800 Prairie Avenue Chicago* (Chicago, 1978).

43) *American Poetry and Prose*, ed., N. Foerster (1934; Boston, 1947), p. 356.

44) Frank Lloyd Wright, "In the Cause of Architecture," in *Frank Lloyd Wright on Architecture*, ed., Frederick Gutheim (New York: Duell, Sloan and Pearce, 1941), p. 34.

45) Sigfried Giedion, *Space Time and Architecture* (1941; Cambridge, MA: Harvard University Press, 1967), pp. 401ff.

46) Adams, *Jefferson's Monticello*, p. 50.

47) Frank Lloyd Wright, *The Natural House* (1954; New York: 1970), p. 32.

48) Wright, *The Natural House*, pp. 15-16.

49) Grant Carpenter Manson, *Frank Lloyd Wright to 1910* (New York: Van Nostrand Reinhold, 1958).

50) Frank Lloyd Wright's drawings were first published in Europe in *Ausgeführte Bauten und Entwürfe von Frank Lloyd Wright* (Berlin: Ernst Wasmuth, 1910). The next year Wasmuth published a book of interior and exterior photographs and plans of Wright's work, with a text by C.R. Ashbee. *Frank Lloyd Wright: Ausgeführte Bauten* (Berlin: Verlegt bei Ernst Wasmuth A. G., 1911).

51) Christian Norberg-Schulz, *Il mondo dell'architettura*. (Milan 1986), pp. 141, 153.

52) Henry-Russell Hitchcock, Philip Johnson, *The International Style* (1932; New York: W.W. Norton & Company, 1966), pp. 26ff.

53) Peter Blake, *Marcel Breuer: Architect and Designer* (New York: Museum of Modern Art, 1949), pp. 96-97.

54) For illustrations of a collection of contemporary houses by a variety of architects see Paul Goldberger, *The Houses of the Hamptons* (New York: Alfred A. Knopf, 1986).

55) *Leon Krier, Architectural Design Profile* (London, 1984), pp. 108ff.

56) Robert Venturi, *Complexity and Contradiction in Architecture* (New York: Museum of Modern Art, 1966), p. 117.

57) Venturi, *Complexity*, p. 15.

58) Charles Moore, Gerald Allen, Donlyn Lyndon: *The Place of Houses* (New York: Holt, Rinehart and Winston, 1974).

59) *Robert A.M. Stern: Buildings and Projects 1965–1980*, eds., Peter Arnell, Ted Bickford (New York: Rizzoli, 1981). *Robert A.M. Stern: Buildings and Projects 1981–1986*, ed., Luis F. Rueda (New York: Rizzoli, 1986).

60) Robert A.M. Stern, "Toward a Modern Architecture after Modernism," *Buildings and Projects 1965–1980*, pp. 10ff.

61) *Stern: Buildings and Projects 1981–1986*.

62) Christian Norberg-Schulz, *The Concept of Dwelling* (New York: Rizzoli, 1985).

63) Kevin Lynch, *The Image of the City* (Cambridge, MA: MIT Press, 1960), p. 41.

64) Lewis Mumford, *The City In History* (New York: Harcourt Brace Jovanovich, 1961), p. 424.

65) Norberg-Schulz, *The Concept of Dwelling*.

66) Le Corbusier, *Towards a New Architecture* (1923; New York: Praeger, 1970), p. 173.

67) *Colonial Williamsburg Official Guidebook* (Williamsburg, VA: The Colonial Williamsburg Foundation, 1985).

68) Thomas Sharp, *Anatomy of a Village* (Harmondsworth: Penguin Books, 1946).

69) Lewis Mumford, *Sticks and Stones* (1924; New York: Dover Publications, Inc., 1955), p. 3.

70) John W. Reps, *Town Planning in Frontier America* (Princeton: Princeton University Press, 1969), p. 159.

71) John W. Reps, *Cities on Stone* (Fort Worth: Amon Carter Museum, 1976).

72) John R. Stilgoe, *Common Landscape of America 1580–1845* (New Haven: Yale University Press, 1982), p. 99.

73) Stilgoe, *Common Landscape*, p. 98.

74) Mumford, *The City*, p. 424.

75) Mario Maniera-Elia, "Per una città 'imperiale'," Giorgio Ciucci, Francesco Dal Co, Mario Maniera-Elia, Manfredo Tafuri, *La città americana dalla guerra civile al New Deal* (Rome: Guis, Laterza & Figli, Spa., 1973).

76) Stilgoe, *Common Landscape*, p. 96.

77) John Brinkerhoff Jackson, *American Space* (New York: W.W. Norton & Company), p. 203.

78) Edmund V. Gillon, Jr., *Early Illustrations and Views of American Architecture* (New York: Dover Publications, Inc., 1971).

79) Carol Olwell, Judith Lynch Waldhorn, *A Gift to the Street* (San Francisco: Antelope Island Press, 1976), pp. 180ff.

80) Morley Baer, Elizabeth Pomada, Michael Larsen, *Painted Ladies* (New York: E.P. Dutton, 1978), p. 10.

81) Olwell, Waldhorn, *A Gift*.

82) Walter Muir Whitehill, *Boston, A Topographical History* (Cambridge: The Belknap Press, 1968).

83) James Marston Fitch, *American Building*, 1, *The Historical Forces That Shaped It* (Boston: Houghton Mifflin Company, 1966), p. 121.

84) Jackson, *American Space*, pp. 84ff.

85) Margot Gayle, Edward V. Gillon, Jr., *Cast Iron Architecture in New York* (New York: Dover Publications, Inc., 1974).

86) Daniel D. Badger, *Badger's Illustrated Catalogue of Cast-Iron Architecture* (New York: Dover Publications, Inc., 1981).

87) Sigfried Giedion, *Mechanization Takes Command* (1948; New York: W.W. Norton & Company), p. 329.

88) Gayle, Gillon, *Cast Iron*.

89) Gunnar Bugge, Christian Norberg-Schulz, *Stag og Laft: Early Wooden Architecture in Norway* (Oslo: Byggekunst Norske Arkitekters Landsforbund, 1969).

90) Badger, *Badger's Illustrated Catalogue*.

91) Carl W. Condit, *The Chicago School of Architecture* (Chicago: University of Chicago Press, 1964), pp. 80ff.

92) Louis H. Sullivan, *The Autobiography of an Idea* (1924; New York: Dover Publications, Inc., 1956), pp. 196ff.

93) Donald Hoffmann, "Chicago Architecture: The Other Side," *American Architecture: Innovation and Tradition* (New York: Rizzoli, 1986), p. 107.

94) Louis H. Sullivan, *Kindergarten Chats* (New York: Wittenborn, 1947), p. 111.

95) Sullivan, *Kindergarten Chats*, p. 202.
96) Condit, *The Chicago School*, passim.
97) Sullivan, *Kindergarten Chats*, pp. 202ff.
98) Jackson, *American Space*, p. 212.
99) Paul Goldberger, *The City Observed: New York* (New York: Vintage Books, 1979), p. 168.
100) Sigfried Giedion, *Walter Gropius* (Teufen: Max E. Neuenschander, 1954), pp. 227, 229.
101) Lynch, *Image*.
102) Robert Venturi, Denise Scott Brown, Steven Izenour, *Learning from Las Vegas* (1972; Cambridge, MA: MIT Press, 1977), p. 9.
103) Venturi, Scott Brown, Izenour, *Learning*, p. 20.
104) "Tops," *The Chicago Architectural Journal* (New York: Rizzoli, 1983).
105) *A Tower for Louisville: The Humana Competition*, eds., Peter Arnell, Ted Bickford (New York: Rizzoli, 1982), p. 7.
106) Stern, "Modern Traditionalism," *Buildings and Projects 1981–1986*.
107) Sigfried Giedion, *Architecture, You and Me* (Cambridge: Harvard University Press, 1958), p. 26.
108) Le Corbusier, Pierre Jeanneret, *Oeuvre Complète 1910–1929* (Zurich: Les Editions d'Architecture, Artemis, 1937), p. 128.
109) Weber, *Die protestanische Ethik*, pp. 131ff., 172.
110) Norberg-Schulz, *The Concept of Dwelling*.
111) E. Forssman, *Dorisch, Jonisch, Korinthisch* (Uppsala, 1961).
112) Vincent J. Scully, Jr., *The Earth, the Temple and the Gods* (1962; New Haven: Yale University Press, 1969).
113) Frederick Doveton Nichols, *Thomas Jefferson's Architectural Drawings* (Charlottesville; Thomas Jefferson Memorial Foundation and The University Press of Virginia, 1961), p. 8.
114) The axis was blocked by a new building in 1898, by McKim, Mead and White.

115) Pierson, *American Buildings*, 1, pp. 78ff.
116) Pierson, *American Buildings*, 1, p. 250.
117) Pierson, *American Buildings*, 1, p. 239 etc.
118) Martin Heidegger, "Letter on Humanism," *Basic Writings* (New York: Harper & Row, 1977), p. 193.
119) Christian Norberg-Schulz, "Varför Palladio?", *Palladio idag* (Stockholm, 1985).
120) Giedion, *Mechanization*, pp. 329ff.
121) Richard Guy Wilson, *McKim, Mead & White, Architects* (New York: Rizzoli, 1983).
122) James F. O'Gorman, *The Architecture of Frank Furness* (Philadelphia: Philadelphia Museum of Art, 1973).
123) Vincent J. Scully, Jr., "Louis Sullivan's Architectural Ornament," *Perspecta* 5 (New Haven, 1959).
124) The works of Bernard Maybeck ought to be added to those of Furness as an early example of "modern eclecticism." See Kenneth H. Cardwell, *Bernard Maybeck* (Salt Lake City: Gibbs M. Smith Inc., Peregrine Smith Books, 1977).
125) Henry Russell Hitchcock in fact called his book on Wright *In the Nature of Materials* (New York: Duell, Sloan and Pearce, 1942).
126) More interesting are Eero Saarinen's attempts at creating a "meaningful" architecture. See *Eero Saarinen on His Work*, ed., Aline B. Saarinen (New Haven: Yale University Press, 1962).
127) The main source is Kahn's text "Order is," first published in *Perspecta* 3, 1955, then in Vincent J. Scully, Jr., *Louis I. Kahn* (New York: George Braziller, 1962), p. 113, and in Wurman, *What Will Be*.
128) Christian Norberg-Schulz, "Kahn, Heidegger and the Language of Architecture," *Oppositions* 18 (Cambridge, MA: MIT Press, 1979).
129) Scully, *Louis I. Kahn*, p. 25.
130) Venturi, *Complexity*.
131) Venturi, *Complexity*, pp. 18ff.

132) Venturi's "rediscovery" of architectural form has been anticipated in the writings of art historians such as Wolfflin, Riegel, Frankl, Brinckmann, Frey, Sedlmayr, and Wittkower. See Christian Norberg-Schulz, *Intentions in Architecture* (Oslo: Universitetsforlaget; London: Allen & Unwin, Ltd., 1963).
133) *Global Architecture* 39 (Tokyo, 1976).
134) Robert Venturi, "Une defination de l'architecture comme abri decore," *L'architecture d'aujourd'hui 197* (Paris, 1978).
135) Venturi, *Complexity*, pp. 46ff.
136) *Michael Graves: Buildings and Projects 1966–1981*, eds., Karen V. Wheeler, Peter Arnell, Ted Bickford (New York: Rizzoli, 1982).
137) Susanne Langer, *Feeling and Form* (New York: Scibner, 1953), p. 97.
138) Le Corbusier's plan for Chandigarh exhibits natural and traditional patterns within an encompassing grid! See Le Corbusier, *Oeuvre Complète 1952–57*, ed., W. Boesiger (Zurich: Les Éditions d'Architecture, Artemis, 1957), pp. 50ff.
139) Giedion, *Mechanization*.